THE ARTHUR NEGUS GUIDE TO
BRITISH PEWTER, COPPER AND BRASS

The Arthur Negus Guide to British

PEWTER, COPPER AND BRASS

PETER HORNSBY

Foreword by Arthur Negus

Consultant Editor: Arthur Negus

Hamlyn

London · New York · Sydney · Toronto

Frontispiece: Eighteenth-century brass standish.
Cambridge Folk Museum.

Published by
The Hamlyn Publishing Group Limited
London · New York · Sydney · Toronto
Astronaut House, Feltham, Middlesex
England

ISBN 0 600 34217 4

Printed in Italy

Photographic acknowledgements

Author 2, 3, 12, 19, 20, 34, 46, 52, 53, 56, 57, 58, 60, 62, 64, 83, 98,
105, 134; Brighton Museum 90, 109; Hamlyn Group Picture
Library Frontispiece, 78, 79, 80, 81, 82, 103, 114, 116, 118, 120,
126; Hamlyn Group-Thomas-Photos 1, 10, 13, 16, 22, 23, 25, 30,
35, 36, 37, 38, 41, 43, 45, 47, 49, 65, 72, 73, 74, 75, 77, 85, 89, 93,
97, 100, 101, 102, 110, 111, 113, 115, 119, 121, 129, 133, 135, 136,
139; Hamlyn Group-John Webb 5, 6, 7, 18, 21, 24, 26, 31, 32, 33,
39, 40, 51, 66, 67, 70, 71, 76, 88, 92, 95, 96, 104, 112, 117, 128,
137, 138; Robert Perry 107; National Museum of Antiquities,
Edinburgh 9; Sotheby Parke Bernet, London 8, 11, 14, 15, 17, 27,
28, 29, 42, 44, 48, 50, 54, 55, 59, 61; Cyril Staal 63, 87, 94, 99, 106,
108, 122, 130; Victoria and Albert Museum, London 84, 86, 91,
123, 124, 125, 127, 131, 132.

We are grateful to the following for allowing us to photograph:
Jack Casimir Ltd, The Brass shop, 23 Pembridge Road,
London W.11, Robin Bellamy Ltd, 97-99 Corn St. Witney and Key
Antiques, 11 Horsefair, Chipping Norton.

Contents

Foreword by Arthur Negus

Although antique pewter, copper and brass have become increasingly popular not very much has been written about them. I suppose most people will recognise old furniture, silver and porcelain, but perhaps, in the past, pewter and early bell metal have been neglected.

I have been pleasantly surprised, therefore, in reading through this work to learn of the great variety of objects made in these metals. No doubt this and the fact that many of these objects are still comparatively cheap accounts, in part, for their increasing popularity. There is something here for everyone; and for the interested collector there is plenty of scope to start and build up a worthwhile collection.

Peter Hornsby's expertise and enthusiasm combine to provide a book that will appeal to all, both collectors and novices. The history of the subject, methods of production, local and regional styles and the whole range of domestic metalware can all be found here and the author conveys the excitement of collecting as well as his own specialist knowledge.

This is a book I am most pleased to add to this series of reference books.

Arthur Negus

Chapter 1

Collecting base metal

Interest in base metal, as the alloys of copper and tin, are termed, has grown considerably in recent years. Attractive displays of brass and pewter especially are to be seen in many antique shops and most sale rooms regularly offer base-metal objects at auction.

Almost everything that has at one time or another been made in metal has been worked in copper, brass and bronze and there are a very substantial range of objects in pewter. Copper alloys have played their part in industry, science and agriculture and pewter was to be found in church and tavern.

For several hundred years base metal was to be the main material used in the home where wood could not serve. Our forefathers relied on bronze and brass for cooking, ate and drank from pewter, lit their homes with base-metal candlesticks and came to rely on these alloys for a great range of household duties.

This book looks at British domestic metalware in the alloys of copper and tin. In order to deal adequately with this considerable area the focus has to be narrow. Thus iron work is not included, because of its different technology, use and development, and though Europe has been the birthplace of many of the styles most used in the home, things made on the Continent are outside the scope of the book.

Whilst it is necessary to separate these alloys from other metals used by man in the home we must never forget the debt that is owed to the people who worked in other materials. Base metal is only infrequently innovative of changes in style. Most movements have been ushered in by the inventiveness of other craftsmen; especially the silversmith.

Likewise although we are considering only British domestic metalware, the links with Europe have been strong. In the Middle Ages ours was a universal Christian world. The creations of the nation state, the diversive pull of language and religious schisms have obscured this universality. But many of our designs find their origins in Europe and it is important that we recall our debt to the European masters.

What is the appeal of base metal?

It is never easy to answer such questions. Just why do people collect? Our motivations are always complex and deeply buried. I can only hazard an explanation of its appeal.

Domestic metalware is mostly simple in style and made for use. This is in contrast to most things worked in other materials where a utilitarian purpose is often combined with a decorative theme. Most silver, gold and glass objects, for instance, though they were made to be used were also designed to give aesthetic pleasure to the user.

The virtue of domestic metalware is in its simplicity. In this troubled and changing world this seems to offer, to some people, something stable and timeless. Moreover, whereas most fine-art objects were made for the few to enjoy, base metal was made by ordinary men and women for everyone. It thus has a universality.

Twenty years ago I would never have thought it possible that I would be writing a book on antique metalware. I was a political scientist and economist by training and was then working in and out of Africa. Had it not been for a chance visit to our local sale room in Kent I might still have been so engaged. But on the spur of the moment my wife and I went to the auction and bought a pair of plated egg warmers for 2/6d. We enjoyed ourselves so much that we went back to the sale room two weeks later.

Within two years we had both become deeply involved in the world of antiques and later we opened our first shop. For the last ten years we have been operating from Oxfordshire where we specialise in antique metalware.

Looking back I am not sure just why it was that we gradually directed our interests in that direction. Perhaps it was that I sensed a good commercial opening—or again, perhaps it was the gift of a glass-bottomed pewter tankard!

Dating hypothesis

The story that came with it caught my fancy. It was glass bottomed, I was told, so that in the turbulent seventeenth century anyone drinking from it would still be able to see an attack coming through the glass bottom. My researches showed that it was actually nineteenth century. So were the pair of fine, cross-stretchered Glastonbury oak chairs which I bought as seventeenth century on my third visit to the sale room! We all make mistakes and would that all mine dated back to those early days!

There is no exact answer in matters of authenticity. Of course, an item is either period or not, but in most cases there is not yet a scientific way to prove this beyond doubt. It is knowledge and experience allied with flair that provides the weapons by which we have to make our judgements as to authenticity.

Inevitably, a book such as this has to offer some precision in its judgements, particularly as to period because people want to know when things were first made and when they went out of fashion. But really all such judgements are only working hypotheses for we were not there to see for ourselves. We postulate dates, we categorise objects, we note changes of style and we build up certain helpful rules. Yet never forget that it is we who do these things. The original maker was not bound by our rules. He made what he did because he wanted to or because people asked for it. Old-fashioned objects remained on sale long after the trend-setters had changed to a new style. And somewhere there may well have been a man ten or twenty years ahead of his time making things long before we believe they were first designed.

The danger with all these helpful rules therefore is that by repetition they become entrenched into final judgements. Early writers on pewter suggested, for example, that the broad-rimmed plate did not appear until the 1640s yet now we know, through research, that they were in use eighty years before. Likewise most writers on base metal suggest that medieval objects were made from either latten (an alloy of copper, zinc, lead and tin) or bronze whereas we know that many are mixed alloys or with a very high copper content and that what to us is a clear distinction between brass and bronze was not one recognised in the language of the times.

So treat my judgements with caution. They will be as fallible as those of the next man. Test them with your own experience. Be sceptical; that is the way progress lies.

Starting a collection

What can be done to learn more about base metal and how ought someone to go about starting a collection?

There is no doubt that wide reading, not just of the books in the areas in which you are interested, but on the social history of the times and of other forms of antiques can be most helpful. A great deal of background knowledge can be gleaned from books and the illustrations will help to familiarise you with the different styles and periods.

Yet in the end things must be handled and examined. For this, attendance at specialised sales in the major London sale rooms is one very good way of learning. View the sale, note condition, look at estimates, mark the items you like in the catalogue and those you don't. Then either sit through the sale or get the prices from the auction house afterwards. Then see what prices things made. How much did condition influence the price? Were you right or wrong in your choices as far as prices went? Why did some pieces expected to do well sell for less than expected and on the other hand, why did other pieces do much better than expected?

Six months in and out of sale rooms would be one of the best ways of learning.

Get out and talk to dealers. Most antique dealers like meeting people and talking about antiques. If you find one that doesn't you do not need to go back. Handle pieces in stock, listen to what you are told and measure it up against what you have learnt so far.

Ask around the antiques trade as to who they would suggest as a reliable dealer in your chosen area of collecting. Don't ask a specialist in that area himself as the advice might not be too reliable! Ask about generally and I suspect that sooner or later one or two names will begin to emerge.

Go and see them. Chat to them. Look at their stock. So far you will note that I have not suggested buying anything. Because until you know what you want and have some knowledge to back up this judgement it's best to keep your cheque book in your pocket.

Some people do their buying at auction. Most auction rooms will give advice, but remember that, as with the dealer, this cannot be entirely altruistic as their commission is based on the amount the items make. They are in the business of selling. Remember that they all exclude in their conditions any liability for the descriptions that they give in their catalogues. Though they are bound by the Trade Descriptions Act, I know of no prosecutions of auction rooms yet mistakes are regularly made. Certainly, while the major rooms employ experts in most fields the small provincial auction houses have one or two trained staff who, however well trained they may be, can not cover every field equally well. This is why dealers do occasionally come up with bargains bought at auctions.

Many collectors find in the end it is best to establish a relationship with one or two specialist dealers on whose knowledge and judgement they can gradually come to rely. It is in your favour, however distrustful a view you take of dealers, that they will hope to do business with you, not just once, but over several years. They will know that you may one day plan to sell back to them what you are now buying. But don't expect bargains from specialists. They may or may not be more costly than a general dealer, but they are not likely to sell something for very much less than its market value; not if they know their stuff!

Bargain hunting takes people to the corners and bye-ways of the antiques world. Sometimes the hunter is blessed by success, but usually if a piece is cheap there will be a reason!

Whichever route you choose to collecting get to know the people with whom you are doing business. Many worthwhile friendships have been made this way.

Chapter 2
The metals and processes

Copper, brass and bronze

Copper was the first metal to be worked by man and its discovery lies deep in antiquity. With its low melting point even the primitive furnaces could extract the metal from the ore.

Copper has two disadvantages. It is soft and when in contact with acids or salts it gives off poisonous oxides. Although some kettles were made in copper they were used to heat water for household purposes not for cooking or drinking, and the use of copper in the home was limited until sometime in the seventeenth century when a system was invented for coating the copper with a thin coat of tin. This, whilst it lasted, made the copper safe. Spoons are marked double-whited as an indication that two coats of tin were applied, and I think that it is likely that this system was derived from Holland.

The first disadvantage, softness, was overcome, probably by chance, by the discovery that if copper is mixed with other metals a strong alloy is obtained.

You may from time to time see references to other alloys of copper not discussed in detail in this book. You will see that people speak of 'Bell metal', 'Gun metal', 'Princes metal' and 'Tutania' for example.

In each case this is the name given to a particular alloy. In some cases, as with Tutania, basically an alloy of antimony (a metal not extensively used) with brass and tin, this is a precise description; but in others, as with Gun metal and Bell metal, it is a term which tells us more about the purpose of the alloy than its content, which will have varied from maker to maker.

There are almost no limits to the variations that can be worked with copper as the basic metal. By allocating a particular combination a name we imply a precision which is usually actually not present. In any case even if we call a certain combination by a special name, there is no way of knowing whether a piece of metal is or is not what we are calling it unless it is analysed. We are probably safer to stick to a general term for copper alloys with some zinc – 'brass' – and accept that other unexpected metals may also be present. If we really need to know what an object is made of there are the techniques available to have it analysed, but for most general purposes all that is important is to establish its content in relation to its main constituent.

Tin was the first hardener used in a copper alloy and the resulting metal that we know as 'bronze' was to give its name to the civilisation that developed two thousand years before Christ.

Calamine zinc was the other hardener used from the Middle Ages to make brass.

Each metal or alloy had its advantages. Copper could be easily beaten into shape, but was soft; bronze cast well, but could not be hammered whilst brass could be both cast and worked into sheets of what was to be called 'latten'. Brass was thus the more versatile of the alloys.

The process for making brass was at first an arduous one. Calamine zinc had to be chemically absorbed into the copper in a complicated process which was costly and not very efficient. There was a natural limit to the amount of zinc that could be incorporated into the copper. It was technically possible to reach about 30 per cent of zinc by this method, but early makers seldom achieved anything like this level and many alloys contained both zinc and tin.

With the discovery in the eighteenth century of a way to extract mineral zinc from the calamine deposits brass of a higher, more even quality could be obtained and if required could contain much larger proportions of zinc.

In addition to tin and zinc other metals such as lead have been added to copper. Many mortars of the seventeenth century are of a lead bronze and some early objects with a high copper content actually have both tin and zinc added.

From the late Middle Ages to the early nineteenth century there were difficulties extracting the trace elements from copper ore and these small proportions of other minerals tended to be left within the refined copper. Their complete absence in an alloy is a definite indication that the metal is nineteenth century or more recent.

As already mentioned in Chapter 1 the divisions between copper, bronze and brass which appear to us to be so clear are very much less defined historically.

In English, for example, there was no word for bronze until the eighteenth century; brass and bronze were both termed 'brazen'. Brass and copper products were sometimes called 'battery' after a name derived from the method by which many were raised; by hammering. Cast brass was 'brazen' whereas hammered sheet metal brass was known as latten.

The same confusion between alloys existed in Europe. In Dutch 'copper' or 'copperwerk' applied to both alloys, in France the same was true, 'Laiton or cuivre'; in German the word for brass, 'messing', does not appear until the eighteenth century.

To our forebears all these products were copper based and they did not feel the need to distinguish so clearly between any one alloy and another. It is only after the discovery of mineral zinc that the sharp distinction between brass and bronze arose, when it became possible to make an alloy containing over 30 per cent of zinc.

There were several ways in which brass and bronze could be cast. The most famous, the 'cire et perdue' method involved making a model of the object to be made, covering this with a thin layer of wax and then creating an outer mould in clay by covering the core and wax with a clay coating. By baking the complete mould the wax would run out leaving the space into which the metal could then be cast. There would have been a small wire join between the inner core and the outer clay case to keep the two in position. The disadvantage of this method was that only one object could be cast before the mould was broken up and it was slow. It was especially useful for fine work as great detail could be modelled onto the wax. Many early bronze figures were cast in this way.

For larger objects or things which were more robust and did not need such fine detail another method was employed.

A clay model was made of the object, baked, and then covered with an even coating of clay. Next an outer coating of clay was applied and then removed by cutting the model in half and lifting out the core and its (first) unbaked clay cover. This unbaked clay cover was then taken off the core. The outer mould was now baked and the two moulds put together, using wire or sticks to keep the core in the right position, viz à viz the casing. The metal could now be cast into the mould which was then broken up.

The use of a different technique made it possible to cast more than one object. By the seventeenth century sand casting, as it is called, was widespread.

The moulds consisted of two boxes filled with a mixture of silica, clay, horse hair and other ingredients. It had to be soft enough to take an impression, but firm enough for this to last after the model had been removed.

A wood model was then made and impressed into the bottom half of the mould encased in one of the boxes. The process was reversed in the other box and the two halves if now put together would contain the shape of the piece to be reproduced. If this was a plate or flat object that is all that needed to be done.

If however, the object to be made was hollow, an inner core had to be constructed. There are several ways in which this might have been accomplished. A clay core slightly smaller than the original wood or pottery pattern could have been used. Another possibility is that the pattern was not modelled in the solid, but was itself made in two halves and was hollow. Then the core of clay could be cast into the pattern. By keeping the core in the correct position in the outer sand mould with wire the object could be cast. The excess wire could then be cut away and on some early cooking pots a small plug of this copper can actually be seen.

For open-mouthed hollow objects the inner core could be composed of the sand mixture provided it was firm enough not to collapse when in use.

Where a two-part mould had been used it is often possible to see the lines on the object where the mould came together. If there was much excess metal this was taken off by scraping, but mould lines are an indication of these early casting methods.

In the seventeenth century bronze moulds became popular especially for small objects such as spoons and candlesticks. More costly to make, they lasted well and made possible a much faster rate of casting. There was a trade in both moulds and patterns. Cooke White, a Derby brazier was offering moulds for sale in 1780 for example, and another maker in the same year had on offer a 'neat assortment of brass founders patterns'.

After the casting was complete the excess metal had to be removed with files or shears and the surface rubbed smooth and then polished. Polishing was accomplished on a wheel.

Copper and brass were also used in sheet form. Sheets of latten were hammered out from ingots by hammermen or under trip hammers, often water powered. This sheet latten was by its nature uneven in thickness. It was used by people making battery. They took the sheets and formed them into the objects required by hammering.

In the eighteenth century rolling-mills, at first also water powered but in the nineteenth century driven by steam engines, took over the manufacture of sheet metal. These mills were capable of making a much thinner and more even sheet.

Prior to 1600 although brazen objects were being made in this country much was also imported from the great workshops of Europe; in Germany and Flanders.

The Founders' Guild, responsible for casting and the Braziers' for hammerwork, were involved from the early Middle Ages, but never had the influence of the more powerful Pewterers' Company. The Founders' Guild would have worked with imported copper and Cornish tin or foreign brass ingot. Likewise the hammermen of the Braziers' would have had to use imported materials. In the late sixteenth century under the expansionist policies of Elizabeth the British copper mining industry was founded and subsequently brass was made here for the first time. It is from these beginnings that the British brass industry developed.

Throughout its history casting and hammerwork in Britain were on a small scale until the eighteenth century. The individual master working with one or two journeymen or apprentices. Each piece carefully made by hand using a series of technically difficult processes.

Whereas the British manufacture of 'battery' was on a small scale prior to the eighteenth century the pewter industry was long established and reached its peak in the seventeenth century.

Pewter, the alloy of tin

Pewter is an alloy of tin with a number of other ingredients which have varied from time to time and with the purpose of the items being made. Copper and lead were the most frequently used ingredients.

Because tin by itself is brittle, it is liable to crack under heat and fracture under the strains of daily use. So though domestic articles were made in tin from the seventeenth century to the nineteenth, their importance was limited. Tin was also difficult to cast and thus had a limited application in the home.

By the addition of one or more other elements, it was found that tin could be made to cast easily, hammered to gain strength and was strong and reasonably durable.

The principal additional metals employed were copper and lead. Copper gave the tin additional strength and lead made it cast more easily. In some pewter 'tin glass' or bismuth as we would know it, was added, but proportions were small, usually less than 0·3 per cent. Analysis of antique pewter can tell us what was put in the furnaces, but we quickly learn that there was enormous diversity. The idea that pewterers of the seventeenth and eighteenth centuries worked to a fixed formulae is disproved. They varied the amounts of tin according to its cost and in accordance with the purpose of the object they were about to make. Plates needed a high tin content to make them durable. Flagons and measures which had to be cast were more easily made with a greater proportion of lead. Even given a standard set of formulae the addition of old damaged pewter traded in by buyers and added to the new metal will have distorted the contents of the melting pot.

Analysis confirms that nearly all plates contain more than 90 per cent of tin and indeed most of them have a tin content in excess of 94 per cent. The remaining elements are copper and lead. Copper seldom rose above 1·5 per cent nor lead above 3·5 per cent.

By and large this pattern is true for flagons and tankards. Only when it comes to baluster measures does the proportion of tin fall to below 70 per cent and the amount of lead rise to above 25 per cent. Tavern mugs and regional measures fall some way in the middle between these two extremes.

Traditionally there were three basic standards for pewter. 'Fine metal' with a high proportion of copper; 'Lay' with around 20 per cent lead, and 'Trifle' used for making small items made up of 50 per cent lay and 50 per cent 'new metal'. But in practice few objects analysed conform to any of these standards. There are, of course, exceptional items with a higher copper or lead content, but in general we find that most objects in pewter are predominantly of tin.

Perhaps this ought not to surprise us for in Europe they do not have a special name for the alloy as we do. In France it is 'étain', in Germany 'zinn', in Holland 'tenn'; all translate as 'tin'.

In the late eighteenth century it was found that by cutting down the proportion of lead and copper and including anti-mony, a harder alloy could be easily obtained. Subsequently it was discovered that this metal could be worked in different ways, more in keeping with the new industrial methods then sweeping through British industry. But most items in pewter are still fundamentally tin with other elements to give strength or malleability.

Traditionally pewter was made by casting in a mould. The furnaces were fired by wood until, from the seventeenth century onwards, coal was increasingly used. The tin and lead would have been melted together; the copper separately and then added later. The moulds needed to be coated with a substance to help the tin to run; pumice, carbon; egg and ochre

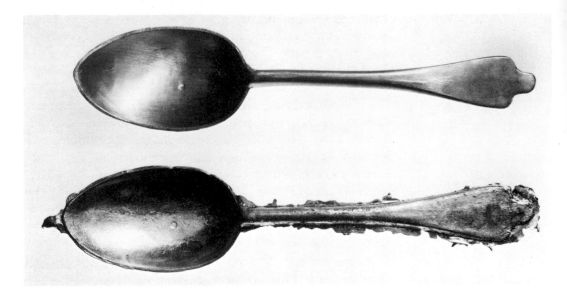

were amongst the materials used. The moment for pouring was crucial, but was measured by the eye rather than scientifically. When the casting came out of the mould it was still rough and had to be scraped or cut to remove the surplus metal. Then, if it was flat ware, it was given to the hammerman for beating. This hammering gave the plate or dish stability and strength. There is evidence that some pewterers tried to save money by not beating their flat ware in the booge (the part of plate that comes between the rim and the bowl, i.e. the rounded sides—these traditionally had to be hammered to give the plate extra strength) and eventually the guilds did permit the sale, for export only, of unhammered plates. These were known as 'Spanish trenchers'—an early case of dumping of inferior products!

For hollow ware the various parts had to be soldered together once they had all been cast. For a simple tankard there were several moulds, one for the body, another for the handle, one for the lid, another for the thumbpiece and hinge. For shaped flagons several additional moulds were necessary. Each part had to be cleaned and then soldered together. When the piece was completed it had to be burnished to an even polished surface. This was accomplished by using burnishers or planishers of steel, agate or bloodstone with a wheel.

To the amateur, pewter is not easy to cast. The temperature of the alloy must be right and the mould must also be at the correct temperature for the metal to flow freely. Yet an experienced caster can, at a glance, know exactly when to pour.

The apprenticeship for pewterers lasted seven years. During

1 Both these spoons have been cast in the same mould. That below is as it came out from the mould, whilst the example above has begun to be cleaned off and finished. The first task of the pewterer was to cut off the surplus metal from where it was poured into the mould and where it spread. Then it is cleaned off using a plannisher and finally polished by further plannishers and then buffed. These spoons were cast by Mr William Kayhoe of Richmond, Virginia, from an old mould. Private collection.

that time the apprentices lived with their master who stood 'in loco Parentis' over them. John Payne of Oxford, for example, had two apprentices Cullis and Mathews living with him in All Saints in 1667.

The moulds used for pewter were generally bronze, but there is some evidence that clay or plaster was used in the more remote areas. For smaller objects stone moulds were also used and Coventry museum has a fragment of a seventeenth-century stone spoon-mould. Many masters worked alone and undertook all the tasks. In larger workshops there was a basic division of labour between the caster, melter, and turner on the one hand and the more skilled hammerman and plannisher on the other. The power for all the work was provided by apprentices; muscle power!

As the number of pewterers grew in the late Middle Ages they tended in England, to organise themselves together into guilds, of which the London Guild was the most powerful and important. In some remote areas, in Scotland and Ireland there were insufficient pewterers so they joined up with other trades to form hammermen's guilds.

The history of pewter in the seventeenth century includes many episodes in which the London Guild, The Worshipful Company of Pewterers, tried to control the activities of the rural pewterers, often without much success. Although they continued their claims into the eighteenth century, the increasingly parlous state of the craft made them less able to enforce their will on provincial workers.

Pewter was never a large-scale industry. Its Masters, journeymen and apprentices worked in small workshops right up to the nineteenth century. It never employed as many people, for example, as pottery. It also never successfully made the transfer from the craft-based trade into factory organised industries that brass was to accomplish in the mid nineteenth century.

Chapter 3

Pewter: the historical background

The earliest British pewter dates back to the last days of the Roman occupation around AD 250, but with the departure of the Roman legions most industrial activity, such as tin mining, declined rapidly. There is no direct evidence of the production of pewter in Britain in the period after the departure of the Romans.

It is not until the ninth century that there is sound archaeological evidence of a revival of tin mining in England, a necessary pre-requisite for the production of pewter.

From the ninth century in Europe there is documentary evidence of the use of pewter. The Council of Rheims (808-13), for example, permitted the use of pewter in church services, but it was not until the 'Council of Westminster' in 1076 that pewter was allowed in churches in England and then only subject to subsequent periods of prohibition.

Thus the first resurgence of pewter in both England and Europe was for ecclesiastical purposes whereas the Romans had put pewter to work in the home.

A number of early chalices and pattens have been found in the graves of prelates and bishops. By 1400 most parish churches had several items of pewter; unconsecrated chalices, cruets (small communion flagons), candlesticks, pyxes (for the host), and christmatories (for the oils).

From the fourteenth century onwards there is fragmentary evidence of the use of pewter in the home, but it was limited to the houses of the nobility and of wealthy institutions.

Gradually the demand for pewter grew helped by a thriving export trade. London was dominant in the late Middle Ages, but other pewter centres were established in such cities as York, Norwich and Coventry. By 1500 most towns possessed their working pewterer some of whom would have been members of the London Guild.

This Guild evolved slowly from the Merchants' Guild during the Middle Ages. The first legal recognition that can be traced was the granting of ordinance in 1348. The Guild received its

2 A fifteenth-century drawing of a pewterer at work. He is casting the body of a flagon.

Royal Charter in 1473.

During the fifteenth century other Guilds were established in York (by 1419), Bristol (1456) and Norwich (1490). In a few smaller towns the hammermen came together with other similar craftsmen like silversmiths, braziers and pewterers to form hammermen's guilds. This was done in Ludlow by 1511. In Scotland and Ireland this was the pattern of development too, with the Edinburgh Hammermen's Guild incorporated by 1496.

It was not until the sixteenth century that pewter began to appear more widely in the homes of the middle classes.

The Tudor period was one of great economic expansion. The growing wealth of the merchants and traders allied with the drive and enterprise of the nobility led to many social changes. Tudor man spent his new found wealth rebuilding his home and refurnishing it; silk hangings for the walls, carpets for the floors, new 'joynt' furniture in the rooms and plate in silver or pewter for the table.

21

John Harrison, a contemporary observer wrote at the end of the sixteenth century of three things 'marvellously altered'. One was the 'exchange of vessel as of treen platters into pewter' and he spoke of even a farmer having a 'fair garnish of pewter on his dresser'. The thesis that pewter was steadily finding its way into the homes of the less well-to-do is supported by the evidence of sixteenth- and seventeenth-century wills and inventories. Two studies of inventories of the period 1550-1600 have shown that at least 83 per cent of them listed pewter amongst the possessions of the deceased. It is true that such inventories were only required by law from those with estates of some substance, but many poorer people also completed the procedure and the inventories show that amongst people of very modest means (owning less than £11 of goods at death), most owned items of pewter.

A good example would be Richard Symmons of Banbury who died in about 1572-3 leaving goods worth £1.9.8d which included '5 pieces of pewter' worth 3/4d.

On the other hand men of wealth often had considerable quantities of pewter. To take an example, from my own home town of Witney in Oxfordshire, Thomas Taylor who died in 1583 had over 200 items of pewter including 'twoo dyssen of plate trenchers' and 'Twoo Flagynn peowter pottes'.

Most frequently found were plates, dishes, chargers and saucers. Including spoons more than 80 per cent of all items listed were used for eating. The only other significant group of articles listed were candlesticks and drinking 'pottes' and cups.

London dominated the pewter trade, but the major cities like York, Bristol, Norwich and Edinburgh all had well-established pewter industries. Most smaller towns would have had one or more working pewterers. Estimating the numbers involved in the craft is very difficult, but it appears that at its peak around 3,500 people were engaged in making pewter. Important as the craft was, it was never a major source of employment.

Even the most successful pewterers worked on what we would consider a small scale, employing one or two journeymen with a few apprentices learning the trade. Most pewterers, especially those in smaller towns, would have worked on an even more modest scale. The workshops were situated in the back of the shop, the pewter being sold from the front. Most pewterers will have made the standard items such as plates, dishes and spoons, but there was also a thriving wholesale trade in the more elaborate articles requiring costly moulds. Most pewterers were likely to have had other craftsmen's work

3 This print is of a French pewterer's shop *c.* 1600. It probably gives a good idea of what an English shop would have looked like at this time.

to sell in their shop. The stock of Rogers, of Malmesbury in 1677 is probably typical. He had the work of three other masters in his shop at that time. It was common practice to buy what you could not easily or economically make yourself.

In the towns the potential buyer would have had no difficulty, but as late as 1700 most people would have had to make a journey to the nearest large town or the local fair to buy pewter.

Pewter was never cheap. In the seventeenth century it cost around 1/- to 1/2d a pound and its second hand value was about 10d a pound. So a set of twelve plates would have cost perhaps 12/3d when an average unskilled man earned 10d a day. Part of the costs could be defrayed by handing in old damaged pewter.

The working pewterer needed considerable capital to start up. He required a furnace for melting the tin, multi-part moulds for casting for each object, many tools for working the pewter including a wheel and also substantial quantities of tin. The will of an Alcester pewterer who died in 1684 tells us something about the value of all this equipment. His furnace was worth over £2, his wheel and tools £4, his moulds £10 and the metal in stock for use £45. A total of over £60 plus his stock for sale which with some brass was valued at £18.

It was possible to set up as a pewterer by buying an existing business or else to start from scratch. Fryer set up in London in 1683 at a cost of £300 and he was in need of more capital quite quickly. In the eighteenth century it appears that between £500 and £1,000 was required to establish an adequately capitalised pewter business, no small sum for those days.

Although the craftsmen were proficient and speedy in their work, the lack of power and the essentially craft orientated methods of working meant that the level of production was low and profit margins easily eroded.

During the seventeenth century the demand for pewter rose steeply and it should have been a time of high profits. But at the same moment that demand was moving steeply upwards so were both the price of tin and the wages that had to be paid.

Pewterers must have faced the early years of the eighteenth century with some confidence. The growth of their trade over the last two decades of the seventeenth century and the universal use of pewter in the home surely promised prosperity. However, although the first twenty years or so of the new century probably saw few changes within the craft the seeds of future decline were already sown.

In theory the eighteenth century ought once again to have been a century of expansion for the population was to double and every new home meant a potential buyer of pewter. It has been suggested that the success in developing the market in the last years of the seventeenth century created some of the difficulties that were faced later. Pewter was not an everyday purchase and it had a useful life of about twenty years if it was well treated. So that the achievement of bringing pewter into almost every home by 1700 left little room for expansion. The success of the last century may have made some impact in the first decades of the next, but by 1730 the rise in the population ought to have brought increased demands for pewter. This would probably have occurred but for the manufacture, and greatly increased popularity of, new cheap substitutes.

These problems had already been recognised as early as 1696 when to protect the pewter industry and ensure fair measure in taverns the House of Commons voted that ale should be served 'but in sealed measures made of pewter' rather than the 'mugs of earth'. The competition of pottery was thus already being felt in 1700.

In the eighteenth century the pottery industry was to expand rapidly. In 1730 there were approximately 1,700 workers making pottery, but by 1770 there were over 5,000; more people involved than there had ever been engaged in pewter. Pottery was cheap, more easily produced in quantity and could be gaily decorated to appeal to the current taste.

Indeed had it not been for the demand from the colonies and other overseas markets the pewter trade might have been in even more serious trouble.

The average level of exports 1700-25 was 4,833 cwt, but this rose steeply between 1726 and 1750 to over 10,398 cwt per annum. The next quarter-century saw further progress as the demands of the American and West Indian colonies increased. Exports reached a peak at an average of 16,799 cwt in 1751-75, and though the War of Independence held back growth over the next twenty-five years by the turn of the century more than 34,000 cwt were going overseas, some eight times the level of export of one hundred years earlier.

The eighteenth century saw some new demand from the growing population, but fierce competition from pottery and later in the century, porcelain and brass jeopardised the stability of the craft, and only the demand for exports saved the trade. Even so, by 1800 the industry was in serious disarray. Techniques had altered very little in over one hundred years. Workshops were still basically small; a master, one or two journeymen and apprentices. Machinery was still manually operated and primitive. The changes brought about by the use of steam engines, machine tools and the other developments of the industrial revolution which were to have an effect on the rest of industry had little impact on the pewter trade. Smaller margins, restricted demand and rising costs all discouraged development. Fundamentally the industry simply did not offer much scope for the new methods.

It is true that the eighteenth-century improvements in communication, the better roads following the turn pike acts and the building of canals did encourage a few enterprising pewterers to develop on a semi-factory basis. Perhaps the most prolific of eighteenth-century pewterers were the Duncombe family who worked near Bewdley. Little is known about their operations and it may be that they were the first to introduce factory methods to their craft. I suspect however, that their large production was partly due to the use of out-workers or to the sub-contracting of work to smaller pewterers, but nevertheless the Duncombe workshops must have been substantial by about 1760.

The dramatic movement of people from the countryside into the towns brought about major shifts in population.

Pewter remained an expensive commodity to transport so that although it was moved by sea, canal and wagon the traditions of the industry had been for local production to supply much of the local needs. In the new cities there was no established pewter industry so that the eighteenth century saw the expansion of the trade to many new centres to supply local demand and Liverpool, Birmingham, Manchester and Glasgow gradually developed into pewtering centres.

With many traditional industries in decline and with the shift in population to the new towns many of the well-established cities were themselves to suffer a considerable decline in the eighteenth century. Norwich and York, two of the leading centres both saw the virtual death of the craft. After 1750 the number of pewterers started to decline and even London was affected. This retraction in London can be illustrated by the number of apprentices admitted to the 'Mystery' as the craft had been called in medieval times. Down from 165 in 1700-1709 to only 35 by 1790-99.

The start of the eighteenth century saw Bristol the leading provincial centre with about 75 masters, journeymen and apprentices engaged at any one time. York came next with an average of about 50. By 1740 the industry in Bristol had hardly changed, but at York it had shrunk to about half. By 1780 whilst Bristol was even more important with about 80 people working, York had sunk to a handful and new cities like Liverpool, Manchester and Birmingham were much on a par. In Scotland the story was the same. The craft remained strong throughout the century in Edinburgh, but grew considerably in Glasgow, a new industrial city, whilst it declined in the older cities.

It thus seems likely that during the eighteenth century the number of people actually working in pewter probably remained unchanged, but that there was a considerable shift within the industry in favour of the new cities at the expense of the older centres.

The crude figures probably disguise a gradual shift away from Master, journeyman and apprentices working in small shops to a fewer number of larger undertakings, with semi-skilled employees, in the new cities able to compete successfully with the smaller traditional pewterers attempting to survive in the increasingly adverse and difficult conditions of the day.

If the second half of the eighteenth century had been bad for the pewter industry the nineteenth century was disastrous. The competition offered by pottery, porcelain and brass became even more severe and the craft was further damaged by the popularity of the new medium: silver plate.

As if these pressures were not enough, the heavy inflation of the late eighteenth century forced up prices and this, together with the demand for skilled men in the new industries led to a heavy increase in the wage rates. The movement towards larger-scale production was aided by rapid improvement in communications following the growth of the canal system and then after 1830, by the success of the railways. Goods made in Manchester or Birmingham could find their way economically to most parts of the country and the smaller old-fashioned rural based industries were to suffer increasingly. This is still basically what the pewter industry was, small scale and local, and suffer it did.

The dramatic decline in home demand was matched by the interruption of exports during the Napoleonic wars and the pewter trade never recovered the lost ground, as their principal market; North America was quickly developing its own pewter industry.

By 1800, outside of London, only Bristol could still boast of a well-established pewter industry, though towns like Birmingham, Bewdley and Manchester in England, Edinburgh and Glasgow in Scotland and Cork and Dublin in Ireland still had a number of pewter establishments at work.

The introduction of the Imperial Standard in 1826 gave a fillip to the dying craft as nearly all the existing tavern mugs and tankards had to be replaced over a few years. Not only did the introduction of the standard help the trade, but the vast increase in beer drinking which was to follow in the 1870s provided another impetus for those firms which had survived. Beer consumption rose fourfold in the third quarter of the nineteenth century and the demand for tavern mugs, brewery equipment, pumps, washing stands and other items for the tavern trade kept alive a dying industry for a few more years.

After 1800 the bulk of pewter made in the traditional way was made for taverns, except for a few domestic items like candlesticks and tobacco boxes. Apart from this the industry faced an almost complete loss of its traditional markets due to competition from other material.

There was another major change within the industry. Around 1770 several makers found that by including antimony in their pewter and excluding lead they could make a thinner, harder alloy. This was at first used in traditional ways to make cast pewter. Some of the pieces marked 'Hard Metal' and 'Superfine Hard Metal' are made of this tin and antimony alloy.

In the nineteenth century this new alloy began to be used in a different fashion. Pewter was spun from sheets rather than cast. A wooden model, of the object to be made, was constructed. This was fastened by a chock to the lathe. A sheet of the pewter alloy was gripped against the form or master and the wheel spun. Pressure was then placed by the operator, with a brass or steel spinning tool, against the sheet so that it gradually changed shape to take the form of the master beneath it. Naturally this technique could only be used for flat ware or for those hollow objects where the widest part was at the top thus making it possible for it to be removed from the form when spinning was complete. Thus items could be raised from the sheet without any casting being involved and with less metal needed. With items of a complex design they were made in separate parts and then soldered together. Tea pots and coffee pots had cast handles, spouts, lids and feet soldered onto the spun and seamed body. In early hard metal, spouts are often made of cast pewter when the body is of the hard metal.

This hard metal is widely known today as 'Britannia metal' although correctly this is the trade name for an English patent metal, which was granted to Richard Forge Sturges in 1842 for the name and composition of the metal. The use of Britannia metal meant that the old long drawn out apprenticeship could be done away with and less skilled and cheaper more easily available labour employed. It also had the great advantage that such techniques were much more fitted to large scale enterprise and steam and water power could be used to drive the spinning machinery.

The new centre for Britannia metal was Sheffield, though work was also done in Birmingham, London and Glasgow. Many domestic objects were made in this metal, perhaps the best known being the multitude of tea and coffee pots made right up to the 1900s by famous makers like James Dixon and Ashberry; who produced scores of designs. To begin with they chose simple neo-Georgian shapes, but with the changes in taste later in the century, pieces became much more elaborate. It was found that designs could be added to the basic form by using metal stamps to create relief designs. Terminals, handles and knops were made in the representation of flowers, leaves and fruit.

Side by side with many tea and coffee pots in Britannia metal are found sugar bowls and cream jugs and also made in great quantities are salts, peppers and mustards, the latter often with blue glass liners as well as countless other small household objects.

One of the mistakes most often made by beginners is to think that the stock or pattern number beneath a piece is its date. These stock numbers are a sure sign that the object is Victorian even if the number suggests a twelfth century origin!

Britannia metal provided a cheap substitute for silver plate and a new alternative to pottery.

It was bought by the less well-to-do, whereas pewter in its hey-day was found at all levels of society. Britannia metal was definitely 'lower' class; hence perhaps the antagonism that most pre-war collectors had for its 'pretentions'.

London and a few provincial makers still continued to make traditional cast pewter, but the day of the traditional pewterer was really over by 1840. From then on there were only a few firms making a limited range of pewter for the Public House trade and the new industrial companies turning out in quantity cheap thin Britannia metal objects, many of which were subsequently plated. The initial letters E.P.B.M. stand for Electroplated Britannia metal just as E.P.N.S. stands for Electro-plated nickel silver.

The 1841 census listed only 300 persons in London claiming to be pewterers and outside the capital only 72 persons listed this as their occupation. These figures will not include those who thought of themselves as factory workers rather than as skilled pewterers. Many more people will have been working on pewter, but the figures nevertheless give an indication of how fast the decline in the industry had accelerated.

The spectacular rise in the brass industry, the dramatic growth of demand for pottery and porcelain, the demand for silver plate and the inability of pewterers to respond to technical change meant that by 1840 the craft was almost extinct. It was to linger on producing Britannia metal and a few individual pewterers continued to eke out a living in the big cities. But its day had passed.

Chapter 4

What to look for in pewter

Condition and colour

Many collectors at the start buy damaged pewter because it is cheap. It's not easy to put out good money when you are not yet confident in your judgements or fully aware of values. Yet there is little doubt that in the long run this is a mistaken policy for eventually the imperfections will come to grate on you. As you get more experience your standards will certainly rise. Frequently I have heard the lament, when looking at a damaged piece, 'I bought it when I first started'.

The other reason why buying damaged pewter is not a good policy relates to its long-term value. Top-quality undamaged pewter appreciates far faster than the damaged. No collector ought to buy only with investment or profit in mind. Such a person is really an investor who should apply financial rather than aesthetic judgements to his buying. Yet it is still only natural to hope to see a collection, bought with care and effort over the years, increase in value. Should one ever wish to sell, damaged pewter never shows the increase in value which attend good-conditioned purchases. This is true with all forms of antiques and the first rule of collecting, in my view, ought to be to buy the best-quality pieces that you can afford.

It's true that there are exceptions to the rule. I would, for instance, never turn down a Tudor flagon just because it was damaged, but on the other hand I would never look at another plate with a hole.

Damaged pewter is not easy to repair. Pewter has a low melting point and its only too easy to do further damage if too much heat is applied. Many old repairs are unsightly. The work was often given to a passing tinker or the local plumber who used a heavy lead solder. These repairs are not easy to remove.

Even a good professional repair can be obvious. If you have to make good a split in a piece with a good colour or patina, the new metal that is added will be bright and stand out like a sore thumb. The solution is to clean the whole surface which will make the repair less easily seen, but may make the piece look over-cleaned. So the best advice is to steer clear of damaged pewter. My own rule is only to buy items that are exceptionally rare if they need repair. Then one has a duty to see that the damage is stabilised for if it is not made good it will surely worsen in the fifty years to come.

Colour is very much a matter of taste. There are two schools of thought. The first says that when new and while it was in use in the home pewter was kept clean and polished. This approach holds that what is called 'patina' is actually dirt or unsightly oxide and that all dirty pewter ought to be cleaned. This is the general attitude of collectors in the USA and Belgium. In England and in most of Europe the patina developed on pewter through the passage of time is highly appreciated. This second view prizes that soft gleaming grey colour which is actually given the name of 'pewter' in the colour charts.

Very heavily oxided pewter can be unsightly particularly if it has patches of rough oxide lifting off the surface. But equally, a newly buffed surface can be too bright. In the end it is a matter of individual taste and judgement. A heavily oxided tulip tankard is shown on plate 43.

If you do want your pewter clean it may not respond if the oxide is at all thick, to rubbing with a cloth. A standard wadding, spirit-based polish will usually remove a light film of oxide and this type of polish is to be preferred to a creamy liquid as the latter tends to dry in the cracks and scratches and leave deposits.

Should the film of oxide be too thick to remove by polishing with a commercial polish you will have to abrade the surface by using either sandpaper or a caustic solution. It is very easy to damage the pewter by either method. Too rough a sandpaper will leave scratches that cannot be taken out and caustic soda or hydrochloric acid can eat away the pewter to say nothing of your fingers.

So unless you are used to handling dangerous chemicals it is best to leave the cleaning of pewter to someone experienced in the task.

Where you do have pieces cleaned by caustic treatment the oxide will be lifted off but you will be left with a new unpolished surface. This will have to be re-finished by buffing on a wheel.

If you do have pewter cleaned try and leave some part of the original surface untouched. If the whole surface is removed then there is little left other than the style to give a confirmation of age. I have seen what may have been rare and genuine pieces of pewter cleaned in acid all over and then so buffed that not one inch of the original surface has been left.

The best way to have your pewter cleaned is to have it done by hand using very fine emery paper and rubbing away the oxide, but this is slow and costly though in the end more easily controlled and less liable to damage the article.

Fakes and reproductions

In Europe pewter has been prized since the nineteenth century and there has thus been an economic motive for the faking of pewter for over 100 years. In this country pewter was not appreciated or valued until after the first Exhibition at Clifford's Inn in 1904. This was the start of British collecting but few pieces had any great value during the first ten years or so of interest so that it was not until after the First World War that any real incentive to fakers existed. Most British fakes are thus less than sixty years old.

This is long enough for some of them to have acquired a genuine coat of oxide. The most valuable in the inter-war years were, as now, Stuart candlesticks and flat-lidded tankards, and these were the items of pewter most often faked in the early days of collecting.

How do you tell a fake from a genuine article? It is certainly not easy with the handful of good early fakes. An analysis of the metal would probably confirm any doubts, but in spite of new methods of analysis this is still not easy to arrange.

Probably the best advice is to seek help if you come across an exceptionally interesting item in pewter. If you decide to buy first and seek confirmation afterwards make sure that you get a clear and detailed statement from the dealer. He is bound to stand by any description that he offers, but in the sale rooms you are less well protected for most salerooms have clauses in their conditions expressly denying any responsibility for the attributions. In practice, though, most sale rooms will discuss any problems that you may have in regard to a piece bought in their rooms.

If you have bought first and intend to ask afterwards you had best contact another collector if you know one, or go and see one of the few specialised dealers and seek his help.

But the best bet is to try and get help first from someone with more knowledge than yourself. In any case approach a really rare item with some natural caution. Ask yourself why it is so cheap (if it is!) Ask why you were able to find it while other more experienced collectors or dealers were not fortunate before you. Perhaps it has already been seen by others with

4 *Opposite and overleaf:* Two pages from a Catalogue of Reproduction pewter *c.* 1926. Note that the Normandy flagon (nos. 17804 & 17803) are wrongly called tappit hens. The maker used his imagination with nos. 17223, 17339 & 17368, the like of which will not be found in antique pewter.

No. 17804.
Tappit Hen.
6in. high.   7in. high
26 –   31 –
$13.00 $15.50

No. 17809.
Complete as illustrated, 55 – $27.50
Oval Dish only, 11/- $5.50
Jug only – 22 – $11.00

No. 17803.
Tappit Hen.
5¾in. 6½in. 7in. 8¼in. 10½in. high.
26 –   31/-   45 – 55 –   75/-
$13.00 $15.50 $22.50 $27.50 $37.50

No. 17223.
Tappit Hen.
9¾in. high.
50 – $25.00

No. 17333.
African Jug.
11in. high.
70/- $35.00

No. 17339.
African Jug.
11in. high.
84/- $42.00

No. 17368.
Tappit Hen.
8in. high.
38/- $19.00

No. 17222.
Jug.
8¾in. high.
36/- $18.00

No. 17338.
Measure.
½   1   2   4   pint.
4½in. 6½in. 7¾in. 9¼in. high.
28 –   45/-   68/-   105/-
$14.00 $22.50 $34.00 $52.50

No. 17224.
Tappit Hen.
10in. high
50/- $25.00

No. 17210.
Plain Round Plate.

6	7	8	9	9½	10	12	14	16	18in.
6/6	8/6	11/-	12 -	13 6	15/-	20 6	36 -	45/-	54/-
$3.25	4.25	5.50	6.00	6.75	7.50	10.25	18.00	22.50	27.00

No. 17211.
Plain Oval Dish.

14in. × 9 in.	...	34 -	$17.00
16in. × 11¼in.	...	40 6	$20.25
18in. × 13¾in	...	50 -	$25.00
20in. × 15 in.	...	60 -	$30.00

No. 17800.
Fancy Edge Plate.

7½	9	10½	12½	14½in.
13 -	15 -	23/-	40 -	55 -
$6.50	7.50	11.50	20.00	27.50

No. 17801.
Fancy Edge Oval Dish.

8½in. × 6 in.	11 -	$5.50	14¼in. × 10 in.	42 -	$21.00
11 in. × 7¾in.	21 -	$10.50	16½in. × 11½in.	50 -	$25.00
12½in. × 8¾in.	25 -	$12.50	19½in. × 12½in.	70 -	$35.00

No. 17334.
Inkstand.

5 in. base × 1⅝in. high	12 -	$6.00
6 in. ,, × 1⅞in. ,,	15 6	$7.75
7 in. ,, × 2⅜in. ,,	21 -	$10.50
7½in. ,, × 3 in. ,,	26 -	$13.00
9 in. ,, × 3¾in. ,,	38 -	$19.00

No. 17337.
Inkstand.
8in. × 4in. × 2⅜in. high.
60 - $30.00

more knowledge? You can have beginner's luck, but usually there is another explanation! It is greed that most often blinds a potential buyer and depresses that natural caution that ought to be at work.

Post-World War II fakes, that is items deliberately made to deceive a buyer into thinking that they are old when they are not, are generally of poor quality. Recently there have been a batch of heavy poorly-cast high-lead-content pieces with an acid colouring in sale rooms, but an application of common-sense to these pieces ought to lead to their being discounted before a second glance.

More difficult are the reproductions made before and after the war. These were made for sale in gift shops and the like and there was no intention to deceive. There has always been and probably always will be a market for copies of fine things. Indeed, large quantities of reproductions were made between the wars and since, and many of these are now old enough to have attained a film of oxide and some wear.

Some of these pieces are copies of early styles, others were the invention of the makers and bear no resemblance to period pieces. They are mostly well made, but because they are basically lead free are likely to feel harder than most antique pewter and they are usually of a thinner material. They have seldom been turned off as they would have been in earlier times and plates are not hammered in the booge. Look too for signs of genuine wear.

The problem of these reproductions is made worse by the fact that before the war there was no trade descriptions act to prevent makers putting the names of genuine historic makers on their reproductions! So that you can find pre-war pewter with the mark of genuine seventeenth and eighteenth century makers. These false marks include, 'S. Duncombe', 'Bush and Perkins', 'William Eddon' and 'John Trout'. There is also a small group of pewter with the mark 'N.R.' which is sometimes mistaken for a period maker, but which is the 1930s mark, of one of the men making reproductions at the time.

In addition to genuine earlier marks used on reproductions, a number of other marks in the period style were invented. They can sometimes confuse less experienced collectors. Such reproduction marks include 'P & D', 'JA with an anchor', and a group of marks with an Irish harp.

Things are complicated still further by the fact that some greedy people have taken reproduction items and have set out to age them and to give them a false degree of wear in order to pass them off as antique.

If all this frightens the life out of you perhaps I should add that much the same could be written about every branch of antiques. Where things are valuable there are people who will try and make a dishonest living by making and selling fakes.

With some experience it is at least a little easier to tell new pewter from old than it is to distinguish many other reproductions from the genuine article.

It takes time to obtain this experience and few collectors or dealers acquire their knowledge without making some expensive errors. Try to find some other local collector and learn from him and his mistakes.

The dating of pewter

As you will appreciate the dating of any article is not an exact science. Much must be left to individual judgement based on knowledge and experience.

Within ten years our judgements will be reinforced by a scientific analysis of the alloys used. It is already possible to have a small sample of pewter analysed which can tell you something about its manufacture, but at present there is insufficient comparative material for this to have much value and in any case it is not easy to get it done.

How then are we to make our judgements? The areas that must be examined are style, purpose, marks, wear and methods of manufacture.

Let us start with the purpose of the object. What can this tell us about its possible period? For example, you will not find Tudor coffee pots a hundred years or so before coffee was in use in this country, nor are you likely to find a Victorian porringer as these were out of fashion by that time. Sometimes, but by no means on every occasion, a consideration of the original purpose of a piece will tell you something about its period.

Examine it for style. Does it conform to any particular period? Look through illustrations of similar articles. This should suggest a possible date based on style.

Next any marks should be examined. If there is a makers' mark can you read it? Consult *Old Pewter, its Makers and Marks* by H. H. Cotterell and *More Pewter Marks* by C. A. Peal, both maybe available in your local public library. If you can identify a maker you are further on your way to dating the piece. Are there any other marks? Such as capacity marks, engraved coats-of-arms or stamped initials? All of these can add something to one's understanding of the period in which the example was in use.

By now the purpose, style and marks ought all to have suggested a possible date to you. If they all say the same thing then you have made some progress. If they suggest several different periods, then leave a question mark hanging over it and move on.

The next stage is to examine the condition of the item. Look at it carefully. Handle it. Run your fingers over leading edges, open and shut the lid to check the degree of wear on the hinge. If a piece of pewter has been in use for a hundred years or more there must be plenty of signs of this use. It might be possible to find an unused seventeenth-century piece of pewter, but I would not bank on it. Because by and large pewter items and those spun in Britannia metal differ in period and method of manufacture, there ought to be no difficulty in telling them apart. In practice whilst the Britannia metal tea pot is not likely to be confused with the Stuart flagon, there are difficulties with pewter and the spun productions both made around 1800-30 where styles are very similar.

The first thing to look for is the thinness of the metal. If it is rather thicker than with tea pots and the like it may be a sign that sheet metal was not used. Look also for evidence of casting and whether or not the object has been hammered. Another tip is to look at the edges of the object. How are they formed? Has the metal been bent back over itself to form a thicker edge? If so, then it's been spun. For example, a cast plate has a reeding beneath the rim in pewter formed in the mould. In Britannia metal the rim has been turned over and shaped down and with a glass it is often possible to see that this has happened.

To take another example, a bowl, if it has been cast, even if it has not been hammered will show signs of having been turned off. Whereas the Britannia metal bowl will have been made by spreading the sheet of metal over the form and, though this is difficult to see with the naked eye, there will be small ridges across the surface which can sometimes be discerned by running the hands over the piece.

Oxide can sometimes help to tell a piece with lead from another with a high antimony content. Pewter oxides faster because of the lead in the alloy and the oxide tends to be uneven, often erupting in bubbles or patches of what used to be called 'tin pest'. Hard metal with antimony has an even, usually rather darker, colour oxide which is very hard and difficult to chip away and which is much less likely to erupt.

But in attempting to make these judgements do not forget that around 1770-1800 many items were cast in hard metal which had they been spun we would have called Britannia

metal. It's the method of construction that separates these spun items from cast pewter.

If all the tests each indicate the same general period then you can say with some confidence that you have been able to date it. If there is conflict between the suggested dates then it needs further study or someone with more experience.

Let us take a practical example of this method of dating pewter. Look at the wavy-edged plate (Plate 15). A plate is a plate so we can learn little about its date from its purpose, but the style clearly indicates an eighteenth century origin. We will see later that, wavy-edged plates were mostly made between 1730 and 1780.

This plate is made by John Home and by consulting Cotterell we see that he worked after 1749. So far, so good. Now let us imagine you can handle the plate. Has it been cast? Are there clear hammermarks on the booge? Does it show signs of wear? The answer is affirmative in all cases. If you could handle it you would see knife marks on the surface. There are no casting faults or pock marks to suggest a later manufacture and it has been hammered and turned. All of these tests thus confirm that it is probably from around 1750-80.

Take another example; the small saucer illustrated here (Plates 6–7) was out of fashion by the early eighteenth century so it is likely from our knowledge of its purpose that it is before 1700. Yet it has a triple-reeded rim; a style going out of fashion at that date. A small seed of doubt ought to have been sown.

Is the plate hammered in the booge? The answer is no. This reinforces our growing uncertainty. Is it well worn? Are there knife marks? Again the answer is in the negative. Does it have any makers' mark? The back carries a crude London mark in a cartouche but no makers' mark, unusual for an early piece.

Purpose, style, method of manufacture, wear and mark, tell conflicting stories and you can safely say that it is not period.

Not all examples are so straightforward, but most genuine

5 *Far left:* Pewter was well finished. This is the base of an eighteenth-century tappit hen showing the excellent turning used to tidy the base.

6 *Centre:* Triple-reeded saucer with broadish rim. Made in the 1930s as a reproduction.

7 *Above:* The back of the same saucer illustrating its lack of finish and crude London mark.

pieces will tell a consistent story; it's the inconsistencies that ought to raise doubts.

Marks on pewter

Most pewterers marked their wares, but in spite of guild regulations to this effect by no means all the genuine items are so identified.

Marks were in use in the Middle Ages, but though the guilds will have encouraged the marking of pewter it was not obligatory until 1503. London pewterers placed their marks on a touch-plate, but these plates were destroyed in the Great Fire of London in 1666, thus depriving us of valuable evidence of the earlier pewterers.

All those pewterers still at work in London re-struck their marks after the Great Fire and from then on until the end of the craft all London makers admitted to the Guild struck their marks on a touch-plate. The last pewterer recorded his touch in 1875. There are five touch-plates and they contain 1090 makers marks, a good start to identifying makers as London was dominant throughout the history of the craft.

It is probable that other centres used similar touch-plates. It is known that this was so in York, but only the Edinburgh touch-plates still survive. The Edinburgh plates were started about 1600. There are 143 touches, the last struck in 1764.

1 John Jolly, *c.* 1720, Edinburgh
2-4 Seventeenth-century marks of William Eddon, Roger Willoughby and Thomas Cowley
5 Scottish seventeenth-century mark of Alexander Ferguson
6 Compton of London, *c.* 1800
7 John Duncombe, early eighteenth century
8 Burgum & Catcott, late eighteenth century
9 Joseph Morgan, *c.* 1810
10 Typical hallmarks of Thomas Mundy, *c.* 1760
11 J. Moyes, *c.* 1860
12 James Yates, nineteenth century
13 John Home, *c.* 1750
14 James Hitchman, *c.* 1720
15 Pitt & Dadley, late eighteenth century

Howard Cotterell in his monumental work recorded the names or initials of some 6,000 pewterers and assigned marks to many of them. Recently the late C. Peal has issued two further lists of makers, and marks. There are certainly many other makers to be discovered from local records and many more marks to be recorded. Makers' marks take many forms. The earliest tended to be small and simple with a device and initials; later marks became larger and in the eighteenth century often included the full name of the maker as well as some device. Some typical marks are illustrated here.

From around 1630-40 another form of makers' mark was gradually adopted. These took the form of false 'hall marks' similar in design to the silver and goldsmiths' marks which still remain in use. These false hallmarks did not include either a date letter nor town mark and were selected not by the guild, but by the individual maker. There can be little doubt that their use was dictated by a desire to ape silver marks and to bring to pewter some of the glamour and value of the silver-smiths' products. No one will have been fooled into believing pewter was silver, but similar marks may have made people believe that they were comparable in importance. A typical hallmark is shown here. These marks continued in use into the early nineteenth century, but appear less frequently after about 1750.

Pewter had an active life and marks are often rubbed and difficult to read. The use of the index in Cotterell often enables a maker to be identified on the strength of part of the mark alone.

Where a mark is worn or rubbed there are several ways of making it more clear. The use of a lens may help, but it is a strange fact that with very worn marks more can often be seen with the naked eye than with a glass. Photography can sometimes bring out a mark and a tracing on paper or a rubbing made on foil can also help. Perhaps the most effective and simple way of enhancing a mark is to use a lighted candle and allow the carbon from the candle to be deposited over the mark. Then take a piece of translucent sellotape and press onto the mark. Remove and put on white paper and the mark will be clearly highlighted. But keep the flame well away from the pewter; you don't want holes in your plate!

Just as silver had its Britannia standard for higher quality work so pewter had its mark for the best quality. This was a crowned X. At first it was indeed a sign of above average quality metal, but soon its use became widespread and appeared on almost everything wholly devaluing the mark.

Other marks found on pewter include origin marks such as 'MADE IN LONDON', or 'LONDON'. Provincial makers were not above claiming London origin for their work! Other marks on British pewter indicate the type of metal being used; 'HARD METAL' or 'SUPERFINE HARD METAL'.

Owners often marked their pewter and Housemarks were often stamped on pewter. Where an owner had the right to bear arms, that is carry an armorial coat of arms, these were sometimes engraved on to the surface. Colleges and other institutions often marked their pewter in this way and it is sometimes possible therefore to identify the former owner of a piece by the arms engraved upon it.

People also used to stamp their initials on their possessions. Where the initials are two in number, set side by side they are the Christian and surnames of the owner. Where they appear as a triangle normally the top initial stands for the surname and the bottom two for the forenames of the husband and wife involved. So

H

P   I

would stand for Peter and Jennifer Hornsby; remember that the J does not appear until the eighteenth century. Where the initials are two pairs they again usually refer to a husband and wife.

Pewter of standard capacity designed for use in the market-

1

2

3

4

5

6

7

8

9

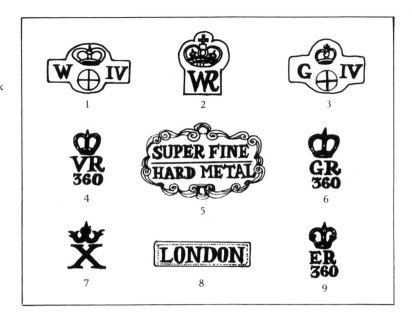

place also often has marks stamped on it by the Weights and Measures authorities. These marks indicate that the measure conforms to the standard of the day.

The earliest mark found is 'HR' or 'hR' for Henry VIII and there are rare occasions when 'CR' is used for Charles I or II. All three marks are very uncommon. The standard adopted under William III continued in use until 1826 and such pieces conforming to those standards are marked with 'WR'. There are a few 'AR' and 'GR' marks indicating Queen Anne and the Georges, but they are not common. Just why it was that the WR mark continued in use is not certain unless it was to confirm the actual standard involved.

On the death of George III a new mark was introduced, 'GRIV' and this was linked with the introduction in 1826 of the new imperial standard. Both William IV and Victoria used the same basic design of capacity marks, with different royal initials.

Victorian capacity marks at first often included a country or town mark, but after 1878 a new style of marking was adopted with a simple 'VR' and a number to indicate the origin and confirming authority. From these numbers it is sometimes possible to identify where a pot was in use, but as numbers were re-allocated from time to time this is not always so. Major cities often had several numbers; Birmingham included 6, Liverpool 147, Manchester 5, Bristol 490, Glasgow 34-36, 59-62, etc. while London had many allocated including 4, 13, 21 and 28.

Edward VII and George V and VI all used this same system. It is possible though unlikely, that tavern pots in use before 1878 were re-stamped with the new system. If this 1878 style of mark is combined with an earlier then the first indicates the date of manufacture, but if only the post-1878 mark is present it is asking a lot to accept that the item was in use in a tavern for many years before being capacity marked. Whilst this is just possible with the 1878 VR marks once the only marks are ER and GR then the piece is definitely after 1902.

In Scotland capacity marking was the duty of the dean of Guild who marked the piece if it conformed to the standard measure with his initials. For example, the mark $\frac{RW}{DG}$ refers to Robert Whyte, an Edinburgh Dean of the Guild in the early nineteenth century. In addition, until 1878 a town mark was also added; in the case of Glasgow for example, a tree. After that the same numbering system that was used in England was adopted.

Decoration on pewter

Most British pewter is plain in contrast to much early European ware. In spite of the general preference for unadorned pewter there have been periods in which British pewter was decorated and some of these pieces are especially prized.

Some European cast decorated pewter is of the finest order. In this country cast decoration is much less common. It is found only on a few pieces before 1620 or so, such as some rare drinking cups with the Prince of Wales feathers cast upon them.

Pewter was also decorated by punching elaborate designs on to the rims of dishes. These punch-decorated pieces first appeared around 1580 and were being made up to the 1680s. Some we know were made in the West of England, but only a dozen or so of these dishes still exist. Sometimes three, more rarely up to five, different punches were used to make the design and they always included a fleur-de-lys.

About the middle of the seventeenth century another form of decoration became popular. It is known as 'wrigglework'. The maker of the piece took a hammer and nail and punched a series of small marks to form shapes or patterns. The effect is similar to engraving, but the lines are not continuous. Most wrigglework pieces are crudely done, for the guilds did not permit the employment of artists and the task had to be completed within the pewterer's own workshop. Many Stuart tankards have this 'wriggled' decoration. There is also a series

8 A group of finely decorated plates *c.* 1700-15. The wrigglework decoration was applied with a hammer and nail by the craftsmen who made the plates. Animals, birds and flowers are popular motifs.

of fine dishes decorated to commemorate the marriage or restoration of King Charles II. There are a number of wrigglework plates which continued to be made up to about 1720. Hitchman was a prolific maker of wriggleworked flat ware. Designs included flowers (the Tulip and Rose being popular), birds (the Dove and Peacock occurring frequently), as well as Royal portraits and other more intricate patterns.

Later in the eighteenth century dishes with line engraving appear briefly though they are very uncommon and most of this type that you will see are Continental.

There are also a few dishes made in this country that are reminiscent of the Nuremburg Latten Alms dishes with their embossed centres and wrythen swirls round the centre of the dish. These appear to have only been made by a few makers around 1730, probably apeing Continental designs.

Continental pewter

In spite of the fact that for long periods the importation of European pewter was discouraged there is much Continental pewter in this country.

Much of this was brought back by Georgian or Victorian gentlemen on the grand tour or by troops after two World Wars.

European pewter is more prized in the country of its origin than it is in Britain. Lead by the Dutch, Continental dealers have been combing British shops since the war. Yet in spite of all their efforts much still remains and every so often a piece of exceptional quality will appear.

Whether out of chauvinism or ignorance, European pewter was traditionally denigrated by British collectors, but much of it is of very high quality indeed, well made and with fine lines. The best of European pewter is equal to or better than our own. If you are attracted by it and can learn to identify it, European pewter can be a rewarding field for collectors. It is however, important for anyone wishing to collect only British pewter to be able to tell the difference.

There are a number of foreign-language studies, but only a few works in English to guide collectors. Perhaps the best is Vanessa Brett's *Pewter* published by Phaidon.

Considerable help comes from the system of marking adopted in most European countries. Much pewter is marked 'tenn', 'zinn', 'étain' or 'Englishe zinn', 'engles tenn', etc. and such marks are obviously of Continental origin.

The crowned rose mark is used in several European countries and where the maker's initials are incorporated within the crown it is a sure sign of European origin. Most eagle marks are German or Austro-Hungarian, marks with a hammer possibly French or Swiss. All marks incorporating three maker's initials and almost all marks with angels are Continental. Likewise small sets of three marks, one incorporating a coat of arms or a town mark are from Europe.

Some of the more familiar themes in Continental marks are shown here.

The principal differences in style between English and European pewter come out when one looks at flagons and tankards. There is a great variety of styles in Europe. Clearly Continental are those pieces with pronounced parrot-like pouring lips, large ball-thumbpieces or with shield or ball feet. Acorn thumbpieces are frequent in Europe and only found on Channel Island pewter in the British Isles. Most cast decorated pewter is European.

Some of the leading shapes of Continental flagons, measures and tankards are illustrated here.

Collecting pewter

What should the collector look for in pewter?

It would cost a small fortune to build up a collection representative of all periods and of all types of objects. It is probably wise to select an area that attracts you, because of the style or shape involved or perhaps the purpose of the goods or their origin.

For example, some people collect just spoons, salts, tavern mugs or plates. Others concentrate on Scottish, West of England, Channel Islands or Irish pewter. Some people collect certain periods, others even try and build up representative collections of one pewterer.

There are a multitude of possibilities open to the would-be collector. I would suggest that two rules ought to be applied.

Continental pewter flagon shapes
1 Flemish
2 German
3 French
4 Swiss
5 German
6 Swiss
7 Dutch
8 French
9 Swiss
10 Normandy
11 French/Belgian
12 French/Belgian

46

Buy items which are in the best condition that you can find and concentrate on the rarest within whatever field you have selected. This probably means that the items will be more costly than buying more broadly, but you are much less likely to come to regret your purchases later if you buy quality items. I am sure it is better to buy less often, but better items than spread your resources over easily found pewter.

It's a costly pastime so make sure you like what you have chosen to collect. Seventeenth-century pewter for example, will naturally be expensive, whereas Britannia metal is still very much undervalued. Many collectors become very knowledgeable about their field and some devote considerable energies to researching the objects they buy. You may not be of this frame of mind, but do remember that buying takes but a few minutes and there is more to ownership than mere possession.

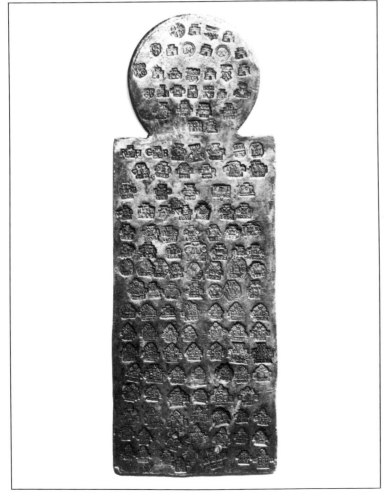

9 The Edinburgh touch-plate which contains the marks struck by Edinburgh pewterers from around 1600 to 1760. National Museum of Antiquities, Edinburgh.

Chapter 5

Pewter for kitchen and dining room

At some point in his history, man stopped tearing at raw meat with his hands and sat down to a lightly grilled fillet steak! Just when the transition took place is lost in the mists of the past, but for the whole of the last six hundred years, and indeed for many centuries before, man has made a ceremony out of eating. That is not to say that the serf in his hovel ate his gruel from a silver bowl, but even in the direst surroundings he used a wooden bowl and spoon to sup his evening meal. The Lord and Lady, in Manor House or Palace took part in more elaborate ceremonies; sharing a bread plate or later a wood, silver or pewter dish throughout a meal of many courses.

We take time off work to eat and in the Western world at least, we eat not just to survive, but as a pleasure. So man has developed utensils and rituals or patterns of behaviour and the kitchens and dining rooms of yesterday and today reflect this.

For the mass of people the diet remained unchanged over centuries. Bread, cheese, ale and less frequently meat or fish were the daily repast. Great quantities of bread and ale were eaten and drunk and these provided the bulk of the calories taken. In winter salted or smoked meat was all that was available and by March this was often a little high; hence the highly spiced dishes so popular to medieval man.

It would be wrong to think that all food eaten before the modern era was plain and simple. Even for the poor, whatever the regularity and paucity of their day to day food, there were feast and saints days to be enjoyed; the roast goose stuffed with apples for Michaelmas. For the rich and powerful, vast meals were served in which the appearance was almost as important as the taste. Twenty courses was in no way unusual, washed down with spiced wine; perhaps the popular 'bastard piment'.

From the sixteenth to the nineteenth century pewter was dominant at the table. It was never used for cooking as it is too soft and has too low a melting point. It appears at the table during the fourteenth century in a few great houses, but it was not until the Tudor economic expansion that it was to appear in

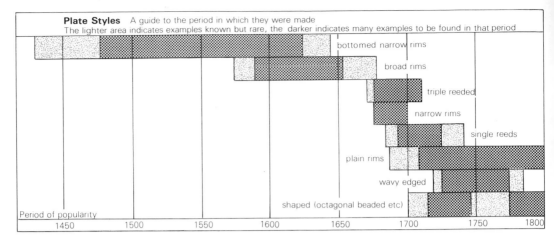

Plate Styles A guide to the period in which they were made
The lighter area indicates examples known but rare, the darker indicates many examples to be found in that period

bottomed narrow rims

broad rims

triple reeded

narrow rims

single reeds

plain rims

wavy edged

shaped (octagonal beaded etc)

Period of popularity

| 1450 | 1500 | 1550 | 1600 | 1650 | 1700 | 1750 | 1800 |

more ordinary homes. The new wealth stimulated a demand for new forms of furnishing and pewter plates and dishes were amongst the first things bought.

Had you been able to glance into a Tudor farmhouse you would perhaps have been surprised at the starkness of the rooms, the simplicity of the furniture, the rushes on the floor and the poor light offered by the rush lights or guttering candles, but your eye would have been caught by the light gleaming off the pewter plates and dishes used by the family and servants alike, stacked upon the Buffet or Court Cupboard in the hall.

It is highly likely that more pewter plates and dishes were made than there are all other items in pewter put together. There are certainly more plates and dishes to be seen than any other forms of pewter.

All medieval pewter is rare and plates are no exception. There were probably several popular styles of plates, but only those with narrow rims and a central boss have survived in any numbers. This central boss, known as a 'bumpy bottom' in the rather prosaic language of collectors, is a distinctive feature of nearly all early plates and dishes until the 1630s. The slope of the bowls does change, becoming more sloping by the sixteenth century and the boss is less pronounced by that time, but it is broadly true that the 'bumpy bottom' plate was in popular use for several hundred years even hanging on in the home until 1670 or so.

Yet the next century, the Stuart era, was to see many rapid changes in taste. In the late sixteenth century a new style of plate made its appearance. This still possessed the central boss, but in place of the narrow rim there was a much broader rim.

In contemporary documents they are referred to as 'new

50

fashioned broad brymmed plates' and are known to collectors as 'broad rims'. By the middle of the seventeenth century the central boss is now starting to be replaced by a flat-bottomed plate. The width of the rim varies according to the size of the plate or dish, but on a nine-inch plate it would be perhaps $2\frac{1}{4}$ inches wide or more and many broad rims had a total rim diameter amounting to over 50 per cent of the total width of the plate. These broad rims are very rare and are amongst the most attractive pieces of British pewter.

Around the time Charles II was restored to the throne, perhaps reflecting a desire for more vivacity after the starkness of the Puritan period, the rims of plates were engraved with lines. At first these reeds were cut into the plate, but later they are cast in relief on the surface. These 'triple-reeded' plates as they are termed embraced both broad-rimmed examples and by 1670 onwards plates with a more conventional width of rim. This style was going out of fashion by 1710.

Another style to appear in the reign of Charles II were the narrow-rimmed plates. These had rims below half an inch, usually with cast reeds upon them and were popular for about thirty years.

Towards the last decade of the seventeenth century another fashion began to gain in popularity. These are the single-

11 On the left a narrow-rimmed plate, on the right a plate with triple-reeded rim. Late seventeenth century. Both show typical traces of oxide which has built up since the plates were in daily use. Signs of genuine wear, the knife marks, are also clear.

12 *Far left:* A typical single-reeded plate.

13 *Left:* The plain rim; the most frequently found form in plates and dishes. This is an eighteenth century dish 18 inches in diameter.

reeded plates, with what we would consider a normal width of rim between the extremes of the broad and narrow rims, but with a single cast reed upon the upper edge. The single-reeded type was manufactured up until the 1730s, but was slowly replaced in favour of plates with a plain rim.

These plain-rimmed plates were to dominate the market from the 1720s until 1830 when pewter plates went out of fashion. The earliest plain-rimmed plates can be dated to around 1695 but they were not numerous until the reign of George I. Plain-rimmed plates are sometimes confused with broad-rim plates because neither has any reeding upon the rim, but the sizes are very different and the width of a plain rim would seldom exceed $1\frac{3}{4}$ inches.

Several other styles of plates were made in the eighteenth century. Plates with six or eight sides were briefly popular in the first decades of the century and a style imported from the Continent, the wavy-edged plates were very fashionable from the 1730s for about fifty years.

Towards the 1770s a revolutionary style was developed. The strangely shaped 'Hot water plates', as they are known, had a plain rim and the plate was mounted on a round hollow base.

14 *Right:* An octagonal plate. Eighteenth century.

15 *Far right:* A wavy-edged plate from the mid eighteenth century. The beading was at first cast with the plate but by 1800 it was often applied later in strips.

The rim had a small hinged flap through which hot water could be poured so that they became table pewter hot water containers, the heat designed to keep the food palatable. They are not very attractive and as they are rather bulky and more costly to make their popularity was limited although they were made into the nineteenth century.

There is no way of knowing just how many plates of any one style were made but it is possible to obtain some idea of the frequency with which they can now be found by analysing the style of plates offered for sale in London in recent years.

Perhaps not surprisingly, plain-rimmed pewter plates which were in fashion for the last 120 years of pewter's popularity are by far the most numerous as the diagram shows. This underlines just how rare the broad, narrow and triple-reeded styles are. It is not possible to incorporate sixteenth-century bumpy bottomed plates as they occur too infrequently to be treated statistically.

Most plates of whatever period are between 8 and 10 inches

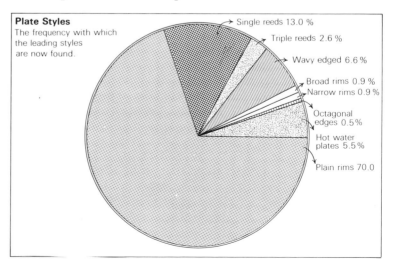

Plate Styles
The frequency with which the leading styles are now found.

Single reeds 13.0 %
Triple reeds 2.6 %
Wavy edged 6.6 %
Broad rims 0.9 %
Narrow rims 0.9 %
Octagonal edges 0.5%
Hot water plates 5.5%
Plain rims 70.0

16 A footed plate or tazza. The beading was cast with the body and is typical of tazza and salts of the 1690-1710 period. Used for serving sweetmeats and confections.

and the general pattern is that plates before 1700 are under 9 inches whilst those that are eighteenth century are usually above $9\frac{1}{4}$ inches in diameter.

Saucers are very much smaller at between 5 and 6 inches. These were not connected with tea, but were as the name implies, small plates for holding sauces. Saucers follow the styles then popular in plates and were widely used up to the 1700s when they seem to go out of fashion.

An unusual plate is the tazza or footed plate of the late seventeenth and early eighteenth centuries. Some of these tazza were used for the host in communion, but most were domestic, used perhaps to serve the popular sweetmeats or sugar confections. They are usually between 8 and 10 inches in diameter and have narrow-reeded rims. They stand on a widening foot.

Few dishes or chargers before 1580 survive. There are a few

17 *Below left:* Broad-rimmed dish *c.* 1650 with less pronounced central boss. 16 inches diameter.

18 *Bottom:* A small serving dish with hollow base for hot water. The spout through which the hot water was poured is in the front. On hot water plates the lid of the aperture fits flush with the plate.

19 *Below:* A pewter tureen by Compton of London *c.* 1800.

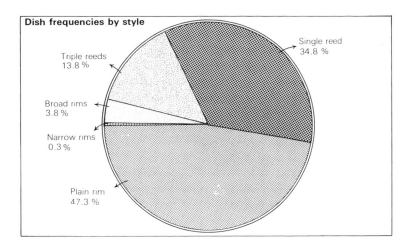

Dish frequencies by style

Single reed
34.8 %

Triple reeds
13.8 %

Broad rims
3.8 %

Narrow rims
0.3 %

Plain rim
47.3 %

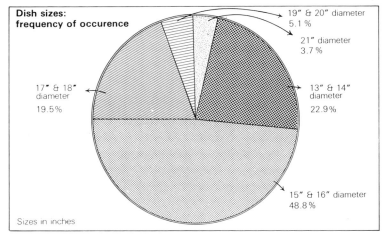

Dish sizes:
frequency of occurence

19" & 20" diameter
5.1 %

21" diameter
3.7 %

17" & 18"
diameter
19.5%

13" & 14"
diameter
22.9%

15" & 16" diameter
48.8%

Sizes in inches

bumpy bottomed dishes, but the earliest style likely to be met in any quantities are the broad rims.

Early records give a range of names for the various sizes and purposes to which dishes were put. The actual purpose of many of these are now unknown and modern collectors have simplified the division by calling all dishes below 20 inches dishes and those above chargers. Chargers greater than 22 inches are very uncommon, but there are a few monsters up to 36 inches in diameter.

Dishes and chargers follow the styles described for plates. The sizes and the relative frequency in which they are found are illustrated.

Broad-rimmed and triple-reeded dishes are slightly less rare than plates of the same style, but narrow-rimmed dishes are most uncommon. Far more single-reeded dishes have survived than with plates so that the plain-rimmed dishes or chargers are less common than one might have expected.

Large rectangular hot water dishes up to 30 inches or more in length were used for the serving of food. They stand on applied feet and have a well for the meat juices. Most are around 1800 and Britannia metal examples appear in the 1820s. These dishes are sometimes called 'venison' dishes even if they were more likely to carry boiled beef and carrots!

One type of dish not matched by a similar style in plates are the oval dishes and chargers so popular in the eighteenth century. These range from 12 inches in length to over 30 inches. Some have plain rims, others are reeded or with wavy cast edges. These may have been made as dishes to go with wavy-edged plates or plain-rimmed plates.

Sets of plates and dishes are not found very often. Originally plates and dishes were sold as garnishes, full services for a dozen or more people. Over the years they have been broken up. Complete garnishes are occasionally offered for sale, but in most cases all that survive of large sets of plates or dishes are the odd sixes or twelves that have managed to remain together throughout an active life. Any number above six are now called 'sets'. A set of plates is more valuable than the same number of individual examples. Plain-rimmed sets are about ten to twelve times more common than single-reeded sets and broad-rimmed, narrow-rimmed and triple-reeded sets are seldom seen.

Pewter bowls are frequently found from the eighteenth century. The average bowl is round, between 8 and 10 inches wide with a small reeded rim and they rest on a flat base. They were used for all domestic purposes. Smaller bowls, on a short stem with a round foot were broth bowls. Many were used in military and naval messes or in other institutions, such as

21 *Opposite:* Fine Charles I pewter flagon with its bun lid and elegant form. *c.* 1625-35.

22 *Left:* Fine broad-rimmed
pewter saucer, *c.* 1570-90.
It has been excavated and
bears traces of 'natures'
gilding; the effect of trace
elements in the soil on the
pewter. Private collection

23 *Opposite:* Rare flagon from
Wigan with wide base,
double-eagle thumbpiece and
spout. By Baldwin *c.* 1770.

24 *Below:* Cast decorated tea
pot after the Portland Vase.
Made around 1800-20.

25 A rare pewter dish with wrythen bossed centre and punch decorated rim. The punch decoration is similar to that found on dishes of the late sixteenth and seventeenth centuries. This dish is probably early eighteenth century. The 'jelly mould' design is taken from Nuremberg dishes in brass. Private collection.

26 An attractive wrigglework plate. Although it has a single-reeded rim it dates from the last years of the seventeenth century, being made by Edward Gregory of Bristol who died in 1696. The naive Lion is typical of the designs on these decorated plates. Below the plate is a fifteenth-century pewter spoon with a diamond point knop. Private collection.

27 Pewter was often bought as a 'garnish' or set, plates and dishes sufficient to fill the needs of the family. Part of an eighteenth-century garnish, here the round plates are matched with wavy-edged oval shaped dishes.

prisons, poor law almshouses and schools as well as in ordinary homes. Beware of bowls with Naval inscriptions as some are later engraved. The broth bowl appears in the late seventeenth century and remained popular into the 1880s.

Porringers, a form of eating bowl, were very popular until the early eighteenth century. Porringers have small round bowls with either one or two handles known as 'ears'. They were ideal for the soups, potages, gruels or stews of the times.

Sixteenth-century porringers, have either one or two ears, whereas most seventeenth-century examples have but a single ear. The ears on early porringers were solid, but on most seventeenth-century examples the ears are fretted or cut and shaped into various designs. Porringers' ears in the shape of dolphins and crowns were popular. Porringers up to 1630 tended to be flat bottomed with straight sides, but later in the seventeenth century porringers with rounded sides, and a central boss were introduced. Around 1690-1700 this boss is disposed with and the sides straighten.

Between 1680 and 1710 a series of fine two-eared porringers appear with cast royal portraits in the base, often with elaborately decorated lids. By 1720 the porringer appears to have gone out of popularity in this country though they continued to be made and exported in large quantities to the USA throughout the eighteenth century.

There are some small rare cups, with either one or two handles used for drinking caudle or punch. These mostly date from the 1680-1710 period and many have a gadrooned body. Loving cups, larger in size, were passed from hand to hand on a convivial occasion. A few loving cups with straight sides and two handles are to be found from the late seventeenth century,

61

but most are rounded in form and are Georgian. They are
bucket shaped with a small stem opening out to a wider foot
and many have ball terminals to the handles.

Until the eighteenth century most people would have carried their own knife to the table. Forks were seldom used until
after 1700 and were seldom made or mounted in pewter.
Pewter spoons, however, were very popular. In relative terms
a large number of early pewter spoons have survived. Many
were lost in wells, sewers or rivers to be found generations later
by archaeologists, or mislaid under the floor boards to be
rediscovered when alterations were made.

Several specialist studies have been made of early base metal
and silver spoons. There are many varieties of bowl shape,
handle style and knops.

Before 1600 bowls tended to be fig-shaped or like leaves, but
in the seventeenth century they become more rounded. There
are many interesting knops to be found on early spoons. Knops
in the shape of a melon, lion sejant, ball, hexagonal, apostle,
maidenhead or seal top were dominant before 1600 together
with a group of spoons without a knop, termed 'slipped in the
stork', or 'sliptops' for short. There were disputes within the
Pewterers' Guild over the use of latten knops on pewter
spoons. There are a few such spoons dating either from the
early fifteenth century or again in the mid to late sixteenth.
These are very rare, but if you are to come across one it will
probably be a pewter spoon with a latten seal-top.

In the seventeenth century the slip tops and apostles con-
tinue to be popular and are joined by other shapes such as the
pineapple or strawberry knops. By 1640 a plainer style, the
puritan spoon arrives, with a flattened handle and a straight

Pewter knops
 1 slip top
 2 acorn
 3 apostle
 4 baluster
 5 diamond
 6 hexagonal
 7 lion sejant
 8 horned head-dress
 9 maidenhead
10 tryfid
11 seal top (simple bell)
12 stump end

Pewter bowl shapes
1 pointed round bowl
   c. 1300
2 round bowl *c.* 1400
3 fig bowl *c.* 1500
4 oval bowl, fifteenth
   century
5 oval bowl, sixteenth
   century
6 round, seventeenth
   century
7 late Stuart bowl

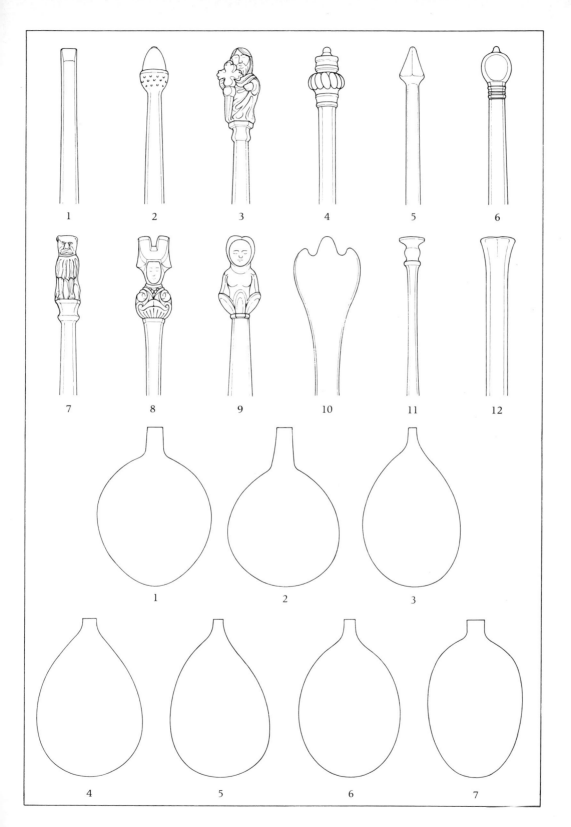

1   2   3   4   5   6

7   8   9   10   11   12

1   2   3

4   5   6   7

end and after the restoration the handles of spoons become even wider and the plain ends of the puritan are shaped and divided to give us the tryfid.

In turn the tryfid developed into the dog nose and from thence the transition was the same as for silver spoons, gradually leading into the Georgian styles largely still with us. Around the period 1680-1710 there are some fine spoons with cast royal portraits, perhaps matching the excellent cast portrait porringers.

During the eighteenth century pewter spoons become rare, driven out perhaps by silver plate or even brass spoons, but in the nineteenth century pewter spoons grow more numerous again and there was a considerable industry in Birmingham, for example, making spoons. Many nineteenth-century spoons are in hard metal.

An analysis of several hundred spoons over the last ten years has shown that only the slip top and tryfid re-occur with any frequency. Together they account for around 70 per cent of all pewter spoons with slip tops being slightly more common than tryfids, probably because of their longer popularity.

All other knops occur less frequently than four times in 100. Such knops are the hexagonals, seal tops, acorns, balusters and puritans. Knops which appear less frequently than twice per

29 A group of salts *c.* 1680-1720. Note the small recess or container.

30 On the left a spice pot. The taller piece is a sugar sifter, the rest peppers. The sifter is 6 inches tall. All except the second piece, a slim waisted pepper which is in Britannia metal, are eighteenth century.

100 include the beehive, horned head dress, lion sejant, maidenhead and stump ends as well as others either unique or known in only two or three instances.

Salt is essential to life. Today, because of its cheapness and easy availability we tend to take it for granted, but to our predecessors it had great importance. The bulk of animals had to be killed each winter as there was insufficient forage to maintain the whole stock. Smoking and salting were the only two ways of preserving the meat during the hard winter months, and salt was needed too, to help make the diet more palatable.

In silver, gold and bronze some wonderful medieval master salts still survive, but salts before 1600 in pewter are virtually unknown. Even in the seventeenth century, salts are rare and never match the magnificence of their more august predecessors.

Salts before about 1720 tend to be made with an inner and outer skin so that the salt does not rest on the outer walls, but sits in a small separate container. Most salts of this period are small for it was a costly commodity. The small bowl was made up into many varieties of shapes; and amongst the more important and attractive are the spools, capstan or octagonal salts. Examples from the 1690s are often gadrooned, that is with raised curved decoration worked onto the surface, or with cast beading on the base. As the eighteenth century developed, salts became larger and the cup salt dominated the last fifty or so years of the century. The nineteenth century saw the appearance of Britannia metal salts, usually with small, round or oval-shaped bowls often with applied feet. Salts in pewter were made into the late nineteenth century alongside their Britannia metal counterparts.

Peppers before 1700 are very rare indeed, but during the eighteenth century they became popular. The baluster shape is the most common style, but during the late eighteenth and nineteenth centuries other shapes such as the 'urn' or 'waisted' styles became popular. Britannia metal peppers are often similar in style to those in pewter, but have thinner bodies and usually a harder oxide; more elaborate shapes of peppers are all nineteenth century and most probably from the second half of the century.

Sifters are sometimes mistaken for large peppers. These were used for sugar or spice or for sprinkling flour. Sifters are less common than peppers and are up to 6 inches or more high. A small group of 'blind' peppers, that is with lids without any apertures are spice canisters for ginger, cinnamon or other

spices, used to flavour food at the table, just as we now use salt and pepper.

Tea and coffee, both introduced in the mid seventeenth century were costly and only drunk by the well-to-do.

Pewter tea pots are rare before the nineteenth century. A few round or bullet shaped tea pots are found from the 1750s but as this style was much copied in the 1920s care must be taken.

Gradually, as the price fell, tea took the place of ale and beer in the nation's diet. From 1800 onwards tea pots were made in Britannia metal. The simple Georgian forms of 1800-20 were replaced by the elaborately shaped and decorated tea pots of the Victorian era. Many hundreds of designs were made; many in Sheffield and Birmingham. The bodies, shaped with floral or patterned decoration, with applied knops and feet in a variety of styles. Pewter tea cups do not appear until the 1890s.

Coffee never attained the importance of tea and was initially drunk in coffee houses. In Europe pewter coffee pots are common, but few are found in Britain until in the nineteenth century when they were made in quantity in Britannia metal. As with tea pots the earlier simple shapes were gradually replaced by the highly decorated Victorian coffee pot.

Many other items were made in pewter for use in the kitchen or in the dining room, but few are of great significance or are found in any quantity.

31 *Above left:* A bulbous tea pot of the late eighteenth century with wooden ebonised handle and knop.

32 *Left:* An early nineteenth century oval tea pot. The body decorated with bright cut engraving, a form often found on silver.

33 *Above:* A spouted coffee pot from the first quarter of the nineteenth century. The lid and spout in cast pewter, the body spun in Britannia metal.

Chapter 6

Pewter for drinking

For several hundred years ale and beer were a staple part of the national diet. Wine, though imported in considerable quantities since the Middle Ages was, because of its cost, only drunk by the wealthy. Spirits were rarely taken until the gin craze of Hogarth's time.

Most ale was brewed at home until the eighteenth century. It was made from malt, yeast and water and was a thick, heavy and nutritious drink. As with most things Shakespeare had something to say about Ale; 'A quart of Ale is a dish for a King!' and a sixteenth-century writer speaks of it as 'thick and fulsome'. Often drunk warmed and spiced as well as cold, it did not store well and would last only up to two weeks. Beer, made with the addition of hops, was lighter and longer lasting. Until the reign of George II most country houses would have had their 'Yeling' house or brew room and their brasen 'woort' pans for ale making.

Only in towns and villages was ale or beer brewed for sale in any quantities. We are inclined to think of beer in the early days being made in and sold from casks, but even in the seventeenth century beer was being exported in bottles to the Americas.

Considering the importance of ale, beer, wine and other drinks it is not surprising that most households had several utensils, many in pewter, for serving drink. One of the problems that customers for most commodities faced was the danger of receiving short measure. Traders, stall holders, shop keepers or tavern owners were only too ready to give less than the legal standard.

There were frequent attempts to establish national standards. Perhaps the most effective were the standards introduced by William III at the end of the seventeenth century. Standards for wet and dry measure, including different standards for ale and for wine were universally enforced in England, and continued in use until the adoption of the Imperial Measures in 1826. The capacity of pieces can help to date

34 *Far left:* The strong erect thumbpiece and knopped lid are typical of this most stately of flagons. Made in the reign of James the first.

35 *Left:* The 'beefeater' flagon with its flat lid and usually twin-cusp thumbpiece came into popularity in the middle of the seventeenth century and were still being made around 1700.

pewter measures. Although measures made to a capacity standard were mostly intended for use in the market place, many were to be found in homes; often used for bringing goods, or drink, back from the market or inn.

A whole range of items were made in pewter for the serving of ale, wine and other drinks.

Flagons, large vessels for bringing drink to the table were in use until the late eighteenth century. Ale and cider measures were popular in the eighteenth century and for the serving of wine the baluster measure remained in service for many hundreds of years. Tankards, both lidded and unlidded, cups, beakers and mugs were used for drinking although the role of pewter was challenged by vessels in leather, horn, wood, pottery or brass.

Although there were flagons in Tudor homes almost no examples now survive. The earliest domestic flagons that can be seen outside specialised museums are those known as James I flagons. These stately and robust flagons were also used in considerable numbers as Communion flagons after the use of pewter in the communion was formally sanctioned in 1602. Many James I flagons are thus ecclesiastical, but Church examples are usually dated or inscribed whilst domestic flagons tend to bear no identification. James I flagons vary in height from perhaps 9 inches to 14 inches. They have slightly tapering sides, rounded lids with a pronounced knop and heavy 'erect' thumbpieces. Early examples have a rounded base, when looked at from below, and stand upon an applied skirt. By 1630 flagons with flat bases appear and flagons without knops and with different thumbpieces became fashionable during the reigns of Charles I and II.

Few seventeenth-century flagons have lips or spouts and pouring would not have been easy. They were not made to any standard of capacity.

Around 1650 a new style became popular. Known as a 'beefeater' from a supposed resemblance of the lid to a Yeoman warder's hat, a considerable number of these fine flagons have survived. They have wide and on a few exceptional examples very wide bases. Most beefeaters have the twin cusp thumbpiece, but there are several variations and there are some examples with knops to the lid.

The next major change in flagon styles to be made nationally was the 'Spire' flagon of the eighteenth century. The Spire is so named because its tall knop is superficially like a church spire. These flagons have stepped lids and their handles are more elaborate than those of earlier flagons. Early Spire flagons are usually tall and tapering, but by the mid eighteenth century the bodies have become broader. The thumbpieces most commonly found on Spires are the chair or scroll. From around 1770, the open chair is almost universal. Spire flagons were made into the nineteenth century.

There are several regional styles of flagons of which the York, 'Acorn' flagon is perhaps the rarest and most attractive. These were made between 1680 and 1740 and have a most unusual acorn body shape. A straight-sided flagon with domed lid was made on both sides of the Pennines during the early eighteenth century and there is also a distinctive 'Wigan' flagon with a very broad base and domed lid. Around 1700 a number of flagons were made similar in style to the flat-lidded

36 *Below:* Spire flagons from the early eighteenth century usually have a slimmer form. This example was made by Christopher Bankes of Bewdley and given to his local church in 1780 when he was its churchwarden. Note the unusual wide base and common 'open chair' thumbpiece.

37 *Centre:* A development from the flat-lidded tankard, these tapering flagons with flat stepped lids were made either side of the Pennines from 1690 to about 1720.

38 *Right:* The tapering form of ale jug. This is a half gallon by Henry Joseph of London *c.* 1780. Note the scroll thumbpiece.

tankards which are discussed later, but much larger than could have been used for drinking.

Measures, unlike flagons, are made to a standard measurement of capacity. That many measures were in private ownership is certain. It was also the practice for publicans to supply mugs and measures for those wishing to buy ale or wine to drink at home. An American commented in 1796 that he often sent to the tap house for his ale and the 'tap house man ... sends his servant with it to your house and also provides mugs for the purpose'.

There are several regional styles made in Scotland and the Channel Islands, but in England, two shapes dominated the eighteenth century. These are the tall straight-sided measure and the squat bulbous lidded jugs, sometimes called an 'Oxford' ale jug.

The eighteenth century ale measure is similar in size to earlier flagons. It has a domed lid and usually a pouring spout. Gallon and half-gallon measures are the most commonly found sizes; the unlidded examples tend to be in smaller capacities. The ale measure was at its peak from about 1750 until the early nineteenth century.

The bulbous-lidded jugs for ale or cider had stepped lids and were also made in ale standard sizes. The half-gallon and quart are the most common. Later in the eighteenth century lidless examples of these measures appear. Most lidded bulbous ale jugs have the open chair thumbpiece whilst a shell thumbpiece appears on many late-nineteenth-century examples. These jugs continued to be produced up to 1900, many by Gaskell and Chambers. Many of the earlier examples have a grid or grating behind the spout to keep out the hops from the glass, but this is no certain guide as to period.

An interesting style of measure is a rare group associated

Pewter thumbpieces:
flagons

Erect (1580s-1640s)
*James I flagons. Later on tappit hens
and pot belly Scottish measures.*

Erect with opening (1630-60)
Charles I and II flagons.

Twin cusp (1640s-1710)
*Beefeater flagons, flat-lidded tankards,
Stuart flagons, and Scottish lavers.*

Rams horn (1650-1710)
*Beefeaters, flat-lids, Georgian tankards
and Lancaster flagons.*

Scroll (splayed) (1690-1760)
*Lancaster flagons, York flagons,
Spire flagons.*

Scroll (1700-70)
Double-domed and tulip tankards.

Chair (1730-80)
*All tankards.
Spire flagons.*

Pierced chair (1740-80)
tankards

Shell (1800-90)
*Ale and cider measures,
Scottish balusters.*

Open chair (1760-1820)
All tankards and measures of the period.

Acorn (1700-1820)
Channel Islands and European.

41 The four main forms of baluster measure. All are of pint capacity. The bud, (top left); the double volute (top right); the hammerhead (bottom left); the ball (bottom right). The slimmer form of the hammerhead and ball balusters is an indication of their seventeenth-century origins.

with the west of England. These have narrow mouths, broad bodies and are always lidless. There are two styles, one being more bulbous than the other. The narrower style is associated with the Fothergill workshop in Bristol. They appear to have been made as spirit measures, but many must also have been used in homes in the late eighteenth and early nineteenth centuries.

The principal thumbpieces used on flagons, measures and tankards are illustrated on p. 71. For every rule there is an exception, but if this is borne in mind these illustrations may help in the identifying and dating of lidded British pewter.

The story of the measure and flagon is thus one of continual change. The baluster, the standard measure for the serving of wine, shows a very different development. With few alterations it continued in service for more than 400 years. Unlike most other forms of pewter it owes nothing to silver or other materials, for the baluster is a design unique to pewter.

Balusters have flat round lids and usually simple strap handles, although in later examples this often ends in a ball terminal. The sixteenth-century balusters tend to be slimmer than the eighteenth-century examples. Over the centuries the thumbpiece, that was used to open and shut the lid, and also the strengthening across the lid where it joins the thumbpiece, varied in design several times. The earliest thumbpiece incorporates a wedge, a heavy bar of pewter running from the middle of the lid to the top of the hinge. In some cases they may never have had a thumbpiece on top, but in others there is evidence of a missing thumbpiece. It is not certain how many genuine wedge balusters there are without a purchase. In the sixteenth century the wedge appears with a ball thumbpiece and from the end of that century until the end of the seventeenth century they often had a 'hammerhead' like thumbpiece.

Because of their rarity it would be well to seek expert advice if faced with any of these early thumbpieces for not only are there modern copies, but genuine early balusters of the seventeenth century with the more common bud thumbpiece have been altered.

The dominant baluster of the seventeenth century, which was also made into the eighteenth, is the bud baluster. The Bud is named after its resemblance to a spring bud. The wedge on the lid is replaced by a small V-shaped attachment. From the second quarter of the eighteenth century another style change takes place and the double-volute baluster with its fleur-de-lys support replaces the bud.

The lidded baluster was on its way out of fashion by 1800 though for a brief time lidless examples were made. These lidless balusters in turn developed into the bulbous measures so common in Victorian times.

The rarest sizes in all balusters are the gallon, half-gallon and the small half-gill. Regard with some caution any half-gills of the bud period or earlier. Our ancestors had little use for such small quantities of wine and spirits were seldom drunk. More commonly found in all balusters are the pints, quarts, half-pints and gills.

The thumbpieces and lid supports of the baluster are illustrated together with the leading Scottish types which are discussed further in Chapter 8. There are, of course, a number of small variations particularly to the later Scottish thumbpieces.

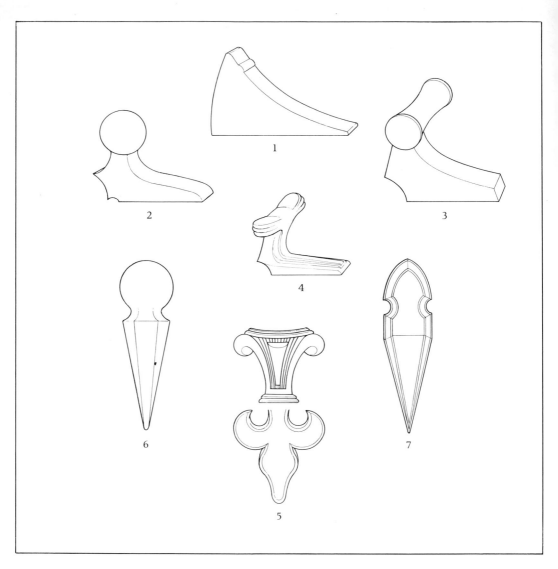

Flagons, measures and balusters were used to bring drink to the table. To actually drink from a smaller more easily held container was needed. Drinking tankards were made in many materials; leather, wood, silver, brass and pottery, as well as pewter.

Tankards before 1650 are very rare. The first group of lidded tankards to survive in any quantity are the Stuart flat-lidded tankards of the 1650-1710 period. They follow the silver style, and are amongst the most attractive and prized objects in pewter.

The Stuart tankard has a flat lid and plain slightly tapering drum. Most have a rams horn thumbpiece although other decorative thumbpieces are found. They were not made to any

Pewter thumbpieces: balusters

1 Wedge – prior to 1600
2 Ball – Sixteenth-century and on Scottish balusters of the late eighteenth century
3 Hammer head – Sixteenth- and seventeenth-century balusters
4 Bud – Seventeenth- and eighteenth-century balusters
5 Double volute – Eighteenth-century balusters
6 Modified shell – Scottish, 1800-70
7 Spade – Scottish, 1780-1840s

42 A group of tankards. On the left and right are double-domed tankards, both with rams horn thumbpieces from around 1700-20. In the centre is the famous flat-lidded Stuart tankard so prized amongst collectors. The serrated edge is on the front of the lid.

capacity, but exist in several sizes. Some of the most interesting have been engraved with 'wrigglework'.

The earliest flat lids have fretted protuberances at the front of the lid, but by about 1700 this had disappeared. The handles of flat lids are simple, straps, and usually end with a spade like terminal.

By the early eighteenth century the flat-lidded style gradually gave way to what we know as the Georgian double-domed tankard. This style first appeared about 1680 and stayed popular until the end of the eighteenth century. On the earliest double-domed tankards the fretted lip can still be found together with the 'rams horn' thumbpiece. By 1715 or so, the commonest thumbpieces are the 'scroll', the 'chair' or the 'pierced scroll'. The plain body of the earliest tankards gives way to a single fillet cast around the body and the spade or flat ended terminal to the handle is replaced by a ball terminal. By 1770 the 'open chair' thumbpiece is most frequently found and by this time the bodies have become taller, and without the fillet.

The next major change in style appeared in the 1730s with the tulip shaped tankard. These had the same thumbpieces found on straight-sided tankards; they also retained the double-domed lid. The open chair thumbpiece became almost universal on tulip shaped tankards after 1760-70. Although not marked to a capacity most appear to have been made in a quart size, though smaller tankards are known.

By 1800 lidded tankards were going out of fashion. A few 'U'-

shaped domed examples were made in the early nineteenth century, but from 1840 the lidded tankard is out of style and only appears again briefly as the sporting trophy of the later part of the nineteenth century.

Lidless tankards were in use from the sixteenth century onwards, but those before 1700 are very rare indeed. A few tall graceful tankards with two or three filets round the body date from about 1660 until about 1720. Most were made to ale standard and were probably for use in taverns.

In the eighteenth century lidless mugs were squatter and spouted examples occur. As the century moves on, the straight-sided mug is replaced with a variety of body styles and handle shapes; the equivalent of the tulip being popular. Most were made to the ale standard. Mugs are rare until the nineteenth century. Many hundreds of thousands of mugs were been made in the decades after the new standards were adopted in 1826, mostly for the inns and taverns though some will have been bought for domestic use. A group of the more popular styles of the nineteenth century are illustrated here. Glass-bottomed tankards are known from about 1800, but most with this feature, sometimes in plain glass, sometimes coloured, are mid-Victorian. Around 1850 a series of tavern mugs, both straight-sided and bellied, were produced with thick, applied brass rims. These must have been difficult to drink from, but gave added strength. Examples are also known with the thick rim applied in pewter and these date from 1880 to 1900.

Ale and wine were also drunk from footed cups and beak-

43 *Left:* A tulip shaped Georgian tankard with double-domed lid and with scroll thumbpiece and ball terminal to handle. The body is heavily oxided.

44 *Above:* A rare late seventeenth century lidless drinking tankard. The twin bands round the body are found on most of the Stuart lidless tankards. The William III capacity mark indicates that it is *c.* 1690-1700. The mark is just below the rim.

Tavern mugs
1 1800-1830 barrel
2 1800-1840 tulip
3 1820-1860 U-shaped
4 1820-1900 pot belly
5 1826-1880 concave
6 1830-1870 cone or
   straight sided
7 1830-1900 flared
8 1850-1900 round handled
9 1850-1900 brass rimmed
10 1860-1900 cone

ers—two styles which developed in the eighteenth century. The earliest cups to survive are a few cast decorated wine goblets from around 1600. Most of the footed cups we find with a short stem, are nineteenth century. The beaker, a straight or tapering sided vessel without a handle first appears about 1690 when it is tall and thin, but later beakers were more squat.

There are more tavern mugs of the Victorian era to be seen in shops than any other item in pewter.

45 Two typical post-imperial pewter beakers with their former owner's initials engraved on the front.

46 A late-nineteenth-century tavern mug with its tamper or wooden form used to remove small dents created by the heavy daily use such mugs faced.

Chapter 7

Pewter in general use

Most of the items in pewter to be found in our forefathers' homes were linked with cooking, eating and drinking, yet pewter filled many other roles in the home.

Before the nineteenth century the candle was the principal source of light. Pewter candlesticks, although nothing like as common as examples in brass or bronze, were made in considerable quantities and most homes prior to 1700 would have had one or more examples. However, only a handful of candlesticks made before 1600 have survived and seventeenth-century patterns are also very rare.

The sixteenth-century candlesticks which have escaped the pressures of daily use and subsequent neglect are nearly all bell-based with a mid drip pan (a round sheet to catch the melting wax and situated at the middle of the stem), much in the style of latten or bronze examples.

In the seventeenth century there were certainly several different varieties, but few of each have endured. The shape most frequently found has an octagonal base, a low drip pan and straight stem. A variation of this form has a scalloped base and drip pan and some examples of each style have heavily reeded stems.

These shapes appeared around 1650, but as few candlesticks bear makers' marks the exact time-span of the shape is obscured.

Less frequently seen are a group of candlesticks with a similar shaped base and mid drip pan, but with a large turned knop in the stem and a candleholder similar in style to the latten candlesticks of around 1600, so this form probably predates the examples with straight stems.

To match the trumpet based brass candlesticks examples were made in pewter both with and without the mid drip pan and these candlesticks were popular in the last forty years of the century.

Towards the end of Charles II's reign candlesticks became generally smaller, the mid drip pan is replaced in position, if

not in purpose, with a large ball knop and whilst most candle-sticks of this shape have the octagonal base there are some with a round base.

The final transition in the late seventeenth century is to a form made familiar in brass; the octagonal based, multi-knopped stemmed sticks. Pewter examples appear to predate their brass compatriots by a few years.

The growth of the population in the eighteenth century and the rising standard of living must have meant a considerable increase in the demand for candlesticks and yet only a very small number of authenticated eighteenth century British pewter candlesticks exist. Such rarity is in marked contrast to the relative frequency with which eighteenth century brass sticks are found. It is very difficult to explain the almost total absence of pewter examples made after 1720. It must be that brass drove out pewter, perhaps because brass was cheaper and new. But whatever the reasons very few British pewter candlesticks of the eighteenth century are known. Those that do exist are similar in form to the brass sticks of the time, usually with octagonal or round bases and knopped stems.

In Europe pewter candlesticks have survived in greater quantities and some of the French and Dutch candlesticks are often mistaken for British.

Towards the end of the eighteenth century pewter candle-sticks began to re-appear. Most have round bases and baluster knopped stems. These continued to be made in substantial quantities into Victorian times. Perhaps the ubiquitous brass

47 *Far left:* There are only a handful of pewter candlesticks made before 1600. This example has a bell base and mid drip pan. Late sixteenth century. Private collection.
48 *Centre:* A fine mid-seventeenth-century octagonal-based candlestick with drip pan. Note the ribbed stem and stepped base and drip pan.

49 *Above:* A ball knop candlestick from around 1690. These are to be found in pewter but are very rare in brass. Private collection.

Pewter candlesticks
1 mid-drip-pan trumpet base *c.* 1650
2 ball knop, late Stuart
3 octagonal-based, Charles II
4 fluted octagonal with low drip-pan *c.* 1670
5 knopped octagonal, Stuart
6 nineteenth-century knopped
7 late Tudor bell
8 stepped round base, nineteenth century
9 Victorian round base with tulip sconce
10 straight sided, nineteenth century
11 rectangular-knopped, late nineteenth century
12 Victorian round base

candlestick was losing its novelty or maybe pewterers, by now in real difficulty, lowered their prices.

It is not easy to distinguish between late-eighteenth and nineteenth-century sticks. The hard-metal examples are certainly nineteenth century, those with a pusher in the stem are probably after 1820. Most oval sticks date from 1820-30 and rectangular-based sticks in pewter are generally mid-nineteenth century. Pewter candlesticks in these Georgian styles were still being made as late as 1880-1900.

Pewter chandeliers and wall sconces are known to have been in use, but though a number of Continental examples still exist few English examples have been found. Brass chambersticks were made in great quantities, but pewter examples are rare and it is likely that the only ones that you will see are late nineteenth century or made more recently.

Before the invention of the fountain pen the only source of ink in the classroom, office or home was from a bottle. Pewter ink stands or 'standishes' with inkwell are often to be seen. Naturally, early examples are rare, but two main styles, made in the eighteenth century, are still to be seen. One form consists of a small square box-stand with one or two drawers in the base. The ink being reached by lifting a small domed lid on top. The other eighteenth-century type is the 'treasury' ink stand, a rectangular box with the lid divided down the middle and lifting in two flaps. On one side the pens or nibs were stored and the other side held the ink pot, paunce pot (which held the sand for drying the paper) and sometimes a small box.

In the middle of the nineteenth century another pattern of ink stand developed. This is a simple round, unlidded pot on a wide round flat base. This type of ink stand often had a pottery

50 *Left:* A small square ink stand with two drawers to hold wafers and nibs. The ink is in a well beneath the domed lid on top. Eighteenth century.

51 *Above:* The two most common forms of tobacco boxes. Both are early nineteenth century.

container for the ink which had small holes set round it to take
the pens and quills. Such ink pots were still in use in schools,
the civil service and offices as late as 1900.

Many items of pewter are found associated with smoking or
snuff taking. There are two main forms of pewter tobacco
boxes. Oval boxes are mostly late eighteenth century whilst
round boxes are generally from the nineteenth century. Both
patterns have concave knopped lids and, like other table
tobacco boxes, pewter examples would all have had an inner
lead press made to hold down the tobacco.

Pewter pipe stands, tampers and small personal tobacco
boxes are still to be found generally dating from the middle of
the nineteenth century.

Pewter snuff boxes come in all shapes and sizes, some round,
others oval or square, some boxes are engraved or embossed.
Boxes can be discovered in the shape of a high-heeled shoe, a
woman's leg, books or other curious shapes. Some interesting
Scottish snuff mulls are discussed in Chapter 8. Pipe tampers
and pipe stands were mostly made in brass, but pewter ones
can be found.

One object in pewter whose purpose might, at first glance,
be rather obscure is the 'Welsh hat', so-called for its similarity
in form to the national headgear of Wales. Whilst they are now
often bought to hold flowers they were originally commode
pots.

This form of 'potty' was used inside a piece of furniture. The
user lifted the lid and 'sat down'. Welsh hats were first made in
the seventeenth century and were made for the next hundred
years. The more traditional form of pot, easily recognised by its
familiar shape, rounded with a handle, is more often found in

pottery or china, but pewter ones were in use from 1600 onwards though few still exist. Whichever form was used in the home their methods of handling the waste product left much to be desired!

The standard advice to servants was never to risk carrying the full pot through the house, but to make use of the windows! hence the Scottish cry of *Gardes lou*. Not all potties sat beneath the bed for as a French visitor commented it was common practice for gentlemen, when dinner was over and the ladies had retired to the drawing room, to use a pot, stored in the sideboard.

For the sick, bedpans were also made in pewter, mostly in the early nineteenth century. They were very similar to those still in use today with round bodies and a short wooden handle.

Medical items made in pewter were in extensive use in the nineteenth century. Syringes of dramatic size and unmentionable purposes were perhaps seldom used by the untrained hand, but small pap boats or invalid feeding cups would have been found in most family medicine cupboards, shaped rather like small boats with a pouring lip on one end. They appear first in the nineteenth century and those made by Dent or Maw are late in the century. There are also many reproductions of these pap boats.

Castor-oil spoons, cunning devices, were in frequent use in Victorian nurseries. They are small spoons with hinged covered tops into which the medicine was poured. The spoon had a hollow handle and when tilted the oil or medicine could be kept in place by putting the thumb over the hole at the end of the handle. When the spoon was in place at the back of the child's mouth the thumb was lifted and down went the medicine!

Most homes would have had a pewter funnel. Funnels were used as we still do today, for transferring liquid from one container to another. They were first made in pewter in the eighteenth century and were made for the next century. They are found in several sizes, some with, some without, straining grids, but all fitting into the end of a standard bottle.

A diligent search of attics, junk shops or cellars will probably reveal other objects in pewter used in home in the nineteenth century for a vast range of items were made in pewter. Few played any more than a transitory role in the domestic life of our forebears, but the hunt may yet produce something of great rarity and importance. The pleasures of the chase remain with us whenever we enter sale room or shop for the unique can be just round the next corner.

Chapter 8
Scottish, Channel Islands and Irish pewter

The pewter industry in Scotland developed quite independently from the English trade. Scotland was a poor and very under-populated nation and the demand for pewter was limited by these factors as well as by the fact that all tin used had to be imported; Scotland mined no tin.

In England the gradual breakdown of the Merchant Guild based on all crafts and trades led to the formation of individual craft guilds, but in Scotland few trades were powerful enough or numerous enough to sustain such craft guilds. As a consequence groups of tradesmen with some common feature linked themselves into united guilds. The pewterers were no exception and formed with other tradesmen Guilds of Hammermen. Such 'Incorporations' as they were called were formed in Edinburgh, Canongate, Stirling, Dundee, Perth, Aberdeen, Glasgow and St Andrews. All these incorporations admitted pewterers, smiths and founders. Many other crafts were permitted membership, some a little surprising to our eyes. Amongst crafts generally admitted were sadlers, silver and goldsmiths, armourers, cutlers, glovers and tinkers.

Often only a small proportion of the guild members would have been pewterers. For example, in Dundee in 1587 only one member out of 35 was a pewterer whilst in St Andrews in 1720 there was not one pewterer amongst the 22 members. Membership of the guilds was obtained only after seven years apprenticeship. As a consequence of the low demand for pewter, few centres attracted more than a handful of pewterers, only Edinburgh, before the late eighteenth century, could boast of a substantial industry. The eighteenth century saw the virtual elimination of the craft in the traditional centres like Dundee, Aberdeen, and Perth, where the last pewterers to be admitted to the guilds were in 1746, 1765 and 1771 respectively.

At the time that these older centres were in decline Glasgow was on its way to becoming a rival to Edinburgh.

Pewter continued to be in use in taverns rather later in

Scotland than in England and for this and other reasons the craft took longer to die.

The last Scottish pewterer, James Moyes, did not give up his shop in West Bow, Edinburgh until the 1870s.

As in England, there were frequent attempts to legislate for and enforce standards on those selling liquid and dry goods. Scotland had its own independent standards up to the Act of Union. Even after the Act special Scottish standards remained in use into the nineteenth century.

The traditional Scottish liquid standard was the Scottish pint, based on the Stirling stoup and roughly equivalent to three pints of the English Ale Standard, (actually 60 fl. ozs., exactly three Imperial pints). The chopin, a name derived from the French, was half a Scottish pint and the mutchkin was a quarter-pint (30 and 15 fl. ozs. respectively). The Scottish pint became known as the 'tappit hen', a confusing name as this is also the term given to the most famous of Scottish measures.

Although the Act of Union officially imposed English measures, the Scottish standards continued in use into the nineteenth century and remained legal even after the introduction of the Imperial Standards in 1826. It was not until 1855 that Scottish measures were finally outlawed. Between 1826 and 1855 they were allowed, if marked in their equivalent imperial measure, and you can find a few measures bearing such odd identifications as '3/5th IP' (meaning three-fifths of an imperial pint), or the like. In addition there were various local standards such as the Glasgow and Hawick two and four glass measures and the muckle gill.

Although the story of Scottish standards is a complicated one, measurement of capacity can sometimes confirm the Scottish origin for unmarked pieces and it may also help in dating.

The French influence was strong in Scotland and French styles influenced Scottish pewter. The most famous of all Scottish pewter measures, the tappit hen, is directly derived from the French *pichet* of the sixteenth century. The Scottish *quaich* or porringer comes from the French *equelle* and the pot belly flagons have their derivation in Flanders.

The Scottish pot belly measures are very rare, robust pieces of pewter from between 1680 and 1730. They have an erect thumbpiece, rounded body and a flat-domed lid. The Scottish pint, chopin and mutchkin sizes are the most frequently found, but half and quart mutchkins also exist. Some pot belly measures were made without lids, but make sure, first, that any you come across have not lost their lids during a busy life.

53 *Above:* A lidless Scottish pot belly flagon. The lidded examples are flat domed with solid, erect thumbpieces. Private collection.

54 *Right:* A set of three Scottish tappit hens: pint, chopin and mutchkin. Eighteenth century.

55 The tappit hen on the left has a knop and is called a 'crested' tappit hen. On the right is a Scottish 'Laver' or flagon *c.* 1800. Earlier examples are usually without spouts.

It seems likely that the first tappit hens were made in Scotland in the sixteenth century, but the first examples to have survived are from the late seventeenth century. The tappit hen has changed its shape very little from when it was first made until it ceased to be produced towards the end of the nineteenth century. Few tappit hens have makers' marks and they were never made by English pewterers. 'Made in London' on a tappit hen is a sure sign that it is modern. The tappit hen has a similar lid and thumbpiece to the pot belly, but has a waisted neck and straight body. As tappit hens were made both before and after the Imperial Standards were introduced they can be found in up to nineteen different sizes. The Scottish pint is the most common. Some tappit hens have a small knop on the lid and these are known as 'Crested' tappit hens. The crested examples were only made in the three principal sizes and only the pint is found with any regularity. Tappit hens and pot belly measures often have a small plouk inside the neck. This marked the level to which the vessels should be filled to conform to their capacity. The existence of a plouk does seem to indicate an eighteenth century date for the item.

There are some tappit hens that were made without a lid and there is also a variant made in Aberdeen, but this type is rare and only found in small sizes.

The third style of Scottish measure is called the 'Laver'. This is a flat-lidded measure with a straight-sided body and twin cusp thumbpieces. It takes its shape from a rare English flagon of the 1700s.

Eighteenth-century examples are robust whilst those made in the nineteenth century are more attenuated, often with pouring lip and knopped lid. The term 'Laver' (derived from

87

the French word laver, to wash) is a misnomer for many are to be found amongst church pewter. Others were used in the home, so it may not be a wholly inappropriate name.

The baluster also found its way to Scotland though no Scottish seventeenth-century examples are known. The earliest Scottish balusters, with ball thumbpieces appear about 1770. Later Scottish balusters had first a spade then embryo shell and finally shell thumbpieces. Scottish balusters have an unusual feature, only also found on some north of England measures. There is an anti-wobble rim, a small applied circle of pewter, under the lid which helps to keep it in place. The inner rim limited the give of the lid and its presence is a sure sign that the piece is northern.

Whilst the early Scottish balusters have much the same body shape as those made in England, after the baluster was out of fashion further south in the 1820s, they developed a more rounded form. Three varieties of nineteenth-century balusters exist. One group comes from Edinburgh and has a small flat top to a concave sided lid. There are two Glasgow styles, both with a flat capacity seal on the top of the lid. In the more common style there is a single dome whilst the rarer examples have double-domed lids. Most of these Scottish balusters were made for tavern use, but some will have found their way into homes.

During the nineteenth century several styles of lidless tankards were made in Scotland. Most will have been made for tavern use. There are also local beakers, some of them made to fit into the neck of a tappit hen.

Scottish flat ware is far less common than English plates and dishes, in general, styles and their periods are the same as in the south. The only unusual Scottish flat ware is the single-reeded deep dish, many of these were used in church as well as domestically.

The Scottish quaich or porringer is very rare indeed. Nearly all examples that you might see are Continental for the solid ear continued to be applied to porringers in Europe long after it had died away in Britain.

There are several very interesting types of snuff mulls of Scottish origin some made for the pocket out of deers feet; others for the table, made from rams horn; each mounted in pewter. Durie of Inverness was a prolific maker of these around 1800.

The variety of pewter in England is not matched in Scotland. There are for example no marked Scottish lidded tankards, spoons or salts though it may be that some unmarked examples are from Scotland.

56 A group of three Scottish baluster measures: the rare double dome Glasgow form (top); the slightly concave Glasgow lid form (centre); the more common Glasgow style (bottom). Private collection.

57 A typical Scottish pear-shaped tavern mug of around 1830.

58 A full size Jersey flagon of pottle capacity. Eighteenth century.

There are some very fine pieces of Scottish pewter to be seen in museums including, for example the Stirling Town Measures, a set of straight-sided measures with the Stirling arms on the front with two plain strap handles and the Pirley Pig, the name given to a unique box in the shape of a pig for receiving the fines of members of the Dundee corporation who failed to attend meetings, but the variety of items is generally much smaller than in England or Europe.

Although owing loyalty to the British Crown, through the Dukedom of Normandy, the history of Channel Island pewter owes much to the links with France.

In spite of their small size it is likely that pewter was being made in Jersey and Guernsey, the two principal islands during the seventeenth century and there is evidence that some pewter was exported to Britain.

From the eighteenth century onwards, two distinct types of measures were to be found in use in the Channel Islands, both derived in form from the Normandy *pichet* in use just across the water.

The Jersey measure, usually made to the local Jersey standard, has the same heart-shaped lid, double-acorn thumbpiece and body style of the Normandy Pichet, but the overall form is more rounded. Measures in Jersey are to be found in six sizes from the pot down to the half-noggin. There have been a number of different standards in force in Jersey, but the eighteenth-century pot was roughly equivalent to 92 per cent of an English ale half-gallon and thus gave a pint of roughly 18 fluid ounces compared with the ale standard pint of 19·7 fluid ounces. The Jersey seal for their standard is a GR crowned, which, with variations, was used from 1727 to 1901. Measures were also made in the same capacities in the lidless style.

Guernsey measures have the same lid and thumbpiece and the body form is again rounded, but it is rather more pear-shaped and often has engraved bands of reeding. The Guernsey measures also have a more inverted foot and are not always made to the local standard. They are only found in four different sizes from the pot down to the half-pint. The capacity seals in Guernsey are the rose or the fleur-de-lys. The Guernsey pot was slightly larger than the one in Jersey and was equal to about 96 per cent of the English half-gallon giving a pint of 19 fluid ounces.

Some of the prolific eighteenth-century makers of Channel Island pewter are known to have worked, for part of their lives at least, in England. There is no direct proof that any measures were made on the Islands, although in their study, Arkwright and Woolmer advanced considerable evidence that makes this likely.

Carter and Wingod, makers of Guernsey and John de St Croix of Jersey all worked in London at one time and struck their marks there. William de Jersey and Hellier Perchard who mostly made flat ware and who came from the Islands also worked in Britain, but there were also local pewterers on the Islands in the eighteenth century. Whether or not the Guernsey and Jersey measures were made in England or on the Islands is, in the end, academic for without doubt the style is unique and their capacity confirms that they were made for use on the Islands.

The development of the pewter trade in Ireland is similar to that of Scotland, although there was no direct Continental influence at work.

Ireland was also a poor nation and the demand for pewter was never strong enough to sustain sufficient pewterers to support separate pewter guilds. The Hammermen came together in multi-craft guilds, in Dublin, Cork and Youghal. The Incorporation is known to have been working in Dublin as early as 1556 and the guilds in Cork and Youghal were both active in the seventeenth century.

The general pattern of development in Ireland is similar to that of England and Scotland: the industry grew rapidly in the early part of the eighteenth century, but after 1800 fell away.

Most of the pewter made in Ireland follows the same style as English pewter, but there are a small group of pieces unique to Irish pewter.

The earliest is a type of flagon which was made in the first half of the eighteenth century. These have domed lids, sturdy, straight bodies and elaborately curved handles, and stand on very wide bases. Many of the Irish flagons are lipped and there is a small blip to be found placed just beneath the spout. Some will have been church flagons, but others will have been used in the home. They were also made without lids and all are very rare.

The two other Irish pewter forms are more common. One is a baluster-shaped measure without a handle. Slightly more angular in form than their English cousins, they were used as Spirit measures and were made from the pint size down. The smallest of the set, the quarter-gill is convex in shape rather than of the baluster form. They are mostly nineteenth century and rarely have a makers mark. They have been much repro-

59 A Guernsey pottle flagon or measure. Eighteenth century.

60 A set of Irish 'haystack' measures by Austen of Cork c. 1820-40 from quart to gill.

61 Half pint Irish baluster measure without handle c. 1800.

duced so care should be taken when buying.

The same goes for the third and best known shape of Irish measure; the 'Haystack'. This is similar in shape to the small haystacks found at harvest time on Irish farms. These measures are made from the gallon down to the half-gill, in seven imperial sizes. Most of them were made for use in wine shops or taverns, but they were also good general purpose domestic measures. Most were made by Austen of Cork, later the Munster Iron Co. The style appears round 1830 and was still being made in the 1900s. These haystack measures have been reproduced and the problem has been made even more difficult in recent years as someone has marked these copies with false Victorian capacity marks.

There is little to say about Welsh pewter as no pewter is known that was made in Wales and there are no uniquely Welsh forms. On occasions flagons are found with Welsh church inscriptions and in St Asaph Cathedral there is a fine example, probably made in Wigan, with an unusual thumbpiece. But Welsh pewter is conspicuous for its absence.

Though pewter made in England was far more prolific than in the rest of Britain the contribution of these other areas has been considerable. In particular the Channel Island measures and the Scottish tappit hens are world famous.

Chapter 9

The history of the copper brass and bronze industry

Copper was not mined in this country on any commercial scale until well towards the end of the sixteenth century. Yet we know that there was a steady production of cast and hammered metalware from the Middle Ages.

The absence of local copper implies that the ore was imported and we know that this is what happened. The only local source of supply of brass or copper came from scrap metal. There is no doubt that this restricted the development of our local metalware industries and that much of the demand in this country was filled by exports from the great European centres right into the early eighteenth century.

It seems likely that most of the early work carried out in this country was in bronze, whilst when brass was worked it would have been imported in sheet or ingot form to be worked here.

Because of the links between this country and Europe in taste, style and even the alloys, it is not easy to state with certainty which items were cast over here or which were imported.

In any case the level of production must have been very small and few pieces from these periods are ever to be seen outside of museums. British manufacture would have been on a small scale, individual craftsmen, often itinerant workers, moving from church to church to cast bells, and then perhaps making a few mortars or pots for the manor house.

The position in Europe was very different. From the tenth century onwards Germany was dominant in the production of copper though the ore was also mined in Sweden, Hungary and Russia.

The largest most productive mines were near Mansfield in Germany and copper was taken from there to the centres of production, often where the calamine was itself available. From the tenth century brass was worked at Huy and Dinant in the Meuse basin and later Augsburg and Aachen became centres of production. In the fifteenth century Nuremburg became the

62 A copperworker hammering a container into shape. An eighteenth-century print.

most important area of brass and bronze production.

The trade was controlled by the Hanseatic League and the products were sold at fairs throughout the Continent or shipped from ports like Antwerp to the rest of Europe including Britain.

Most early brazen products were, as we saw with pewter, made for church rather than for secular use. The use of brazen products in churches was widespread; for candlesticks, crucifixes, portals, grills, reliquaries, christmatories, pyxes, chandeliers and chalices.

There are some magnificent early pieces, many beautifully decorated with enamels and inlaid with precious stones, or gilded. The workmanship was superb and the whole area worthy of further study, although basically outside the scope of this book.

Brazen objects were also made for home use including candlesticks, cooking pots, aquamaniles, mortars, dishes and objects of adornment like rings, buttons, buckles and seals.

Most of these earlier pieces are scarce and valuable and few are to be seen outside the museums. One category of object that can still be found is the alms dish. Made in Nuremburg or perhaps Flemish in origin they have decorated centres and some have finely worked designs such as Adam and Eve, St George and the dragon and similar scenes. Others a little later, are worked in swirls and fluteings with great dished centres. Some of these may have been used for rinsing the hands before a meal, but most of them were purely decorative.

Up to the third quarter of the sixteenth century this would have been the general pattern in this country. Limited local production and a larger scale import of brazen objects from Europe via Antwerp. The 'Merctores de Dinant in Alemania' had their headquarters in London near the German steel yards and were in control of this import trade.

For military and economic reasons Queen Elizabeth decided to encourage the birth of a British copper mining and copper working industry. She needed ordinance for the re-armament of her ships and armies in the face of the threat from Spain. At that time all cannons were cast in Flanders! Beyond the military needs she was motivated by a general policy of encouraging self-sufficiency at home.

In 1564 discussions took place between the Queen's representatives and those of Haug and Co., a subsidiary of Fugger, a firm which was already heavily involved in British trade. Daniel Hochstetter from Augsburg led the company in these negotiations, which culminated in the incorporation of the 'Mynes Royal Societie' in 1568 and later in the sinking of a mine in what Hochstetter had decided would be the most likely area, near Keswick in Cumberland. Hochstetter was resident in Keswick from 1571 and was even permitted to bring in up to four hundred skilled German miners.

At roughly the same time William Humphrey, the Assay master of the Mint, in conjunction with Schultz of Saxony successfully petitioned Cecil to obtain the rights to mine calamine zinc. In 1565 they were granted the rights to mine the mineral, work battery and draw wire and in 1568 the 'Society of the Mineral and Battery Works' was incorporated. Calamine zinc was found in the Mendips in Somerset and soon afterwards Humphrey set up their headquarters near Tintern Abbey on the banks of the River Wye.

The efforts of both societies were not initially rewarded. Both went through periods of great tribulation. The Mines Royal found that there was not the market that they had envisaged for their copper; many merchants preferring to maintain their contacts with Europe for commercial reasons and their efforts to open up the Cornish Mines were not successful. The Mineral and Battery Society also faced many problems as they lacked the skills for making brass. Their products tended to be of lower quality and though they brought in new blood in 1596 neither mining or processing was properly established by the end of the first quarter of the seventeenth century.

Ingot and sheet metal was being worked at Tintern and in Rotherhythe from whence it was being sent out to be worked by outworkers. British copper was being mined and sold in this country, but the progress being made was very limited. All was to be destroyed in the Civil War, both physically in the case of Keswick, sacked by Scottish troops, and economically else-where with political divisions of Britain separating the mines from the brass-making areas.

The initial effort to establish a British copper and copper working industry was not very successful, yet the need was clearly there. There was a growing demand for brass goods, especially in the domestic area and it was not economic sense to allow this to be filled by European imports.

That there was a very considerable demand for domestic metalware is confirmed by the evidence of wills and inventor-ies of the sixteenth and seventeenth centuries. By 1600 most homes contained several objects in worked copper. The bulk of these being associated with the cooking of food. Sixteenth century inventories examined show that 70 per cent of all homes had brazen objects listed. In the seventeenth century the proportion was even higher. The following table shows the types of pieces most frequently recorded.

Sixteenth and seventeenth century inventories

Classification	*% of total objects listed made in copper, brass or bronze*
Cooking pottes, cauldrons etc	74·1
Skillets, posnets etc	6·2
Mortars	1·6
Skimmers and ladles	2·9
Chaffing dishes	2·9
Candlesticks	9·4
Basins and ewers	2·0
All others	2·3

Thus more than 86 per cent of all brazen objects in the home were involved in the preparation or cooking of food. Only candlesticks also appear in significant numbers in the average household.

Even quite poor men usually had a few pieces of brassware in their homes. John Mason of Banbury for example, who died in 1574 in possession of only £2.11.2d worth of goods nevertheless had 'a bras pane three kettles one bras pot' worth 5/-. Men of substance could have considerable quantities of brassware in their homes. John Clifton of Hook Norton who died in 1683 worth £50 had thirty-two pieces of copper ware including 'three latten basons' all valued at £2.14.4d.

That British production was not yet significant is confirmed by John Harrison who wrote at the time ' . . . of brass bell metal and such as are brought over for merchandise from other countries; and yet I cannot say but there is some brass found also in England but so small is the quantity that it is not greatly to be esteemed or accounted for.'

Throughout the seventeenth century, at the very time when the British industry was trying to get off the ground great quantities of copper alloys were being imported into England. To illustrate this traffic into the Port of London, the cargoes for the month of May 1680 were examined. Sixteen cargoes of battery ware amounting to 149 cwt were imported, shipped either from Hamburg or from Rotterdam. In addition there was 21 cwt of wrought copper, $\frac{3}{4}$ cwt of latten wyre and $5\frac{1}{2}$ cwt of copper ingot all in that month alone. Sometimes shipments could be considerable. In January 1680 Mathew Jasen received 17 cwt of battery from Rotterdam whilst the same port sent John Landfewer $19\frac{1}{2}$ cwt in July of that year.

After 1660 the incipient copper mining and brass manufacturing industry was revived. In 1668 the two Societies were combined into a United Society. Initially their products remained low quality and imports as we have seen continued apace. The United Society never reopened the Keswick mines as the cost was thought to be too high. With little copper being mined in the country the supplies for the United Societies and other works had to be imported yet at this time the Society was trying to ban the import of copper to speed up the development of mining here. When eventually, for a brief time, they were successful, the effect was the reverse of what they planned for the absence of alloys to work killed off the incipient brass making industry. For a short time all finished products on the market were imported.

In spite of the monopoly of the United Society other enterprises were started. In Wandsworth in 1671 a Flemish family set out successfully to make brass plate for kettles and frying pans and works were soon to be found in Newcastle-under-Lyme, Coalbrookdale, Studley and Birmingham.

It is important to remember that even though the number of specialised brass works was limited in the late seventeenth century there were many individual masters working in the towns. In Chipping Norton for example, there were five braziers at work in the late seventeenth century. In many cases these men also worked pewter. Such a well-known pewterer as John Payne of Oxford, Mayor of the City in 1687 sometimes listed his occupation as brazier.

The exclusive right to mine held by the Crown was surrendered in 1689 and this stimulated the hunt for calamine zinc and for exploitable copper. The last decades of the seventeenth century saw steady improvements in techniques and a gradual expansion of production though imports remained high.

One of the main reasons why the British industry was less than successful in its first hundred years was the difficulty in bringing together the copper and calamine to make a brass of even quality. Though these skills had been known in Europe from the thirteenth century or even earlier they were not part of the British traditions.

Brass was made at this time by the cementation process, it was undertaken in circular domed furnaces lined with fire bricks. The furnace was filled with pots each holding 40 lb of charcoal mixed and riddled with 100 lb of calamine; then two gallons of water were added. To this mixture they added 66 lb of copper shot. The firing of this mixture would last 10 to 12 hours and involve the use of $3\frac{1}{2}$ cwt of coal. The weakness of this method was that fusion between the two metals was erratic and often uneven as it could not be stirred. There was no access until the process was complete, so very variable brass resulted.

It can be seen that substantial amounts of both calamine and coal were needed to make 1 cwt of brass. In the eighteenth century calamine was being extracted in Derbyshire, Flintshire and in Somerset. The demand for calamine grew apace with the increasing production of brass. From Derby for example, 40 tons was taken out around 1746 but by 1796 the quantity had grown to over 1,500 tons per annum.

The eighteenth century saw rapid progress. In 1704 Abraham Darby opened the Baptist Mills near Bristol and set in train the great period of growth in the British brass industry. However he found the process of casting in brass too slow and tried to find a way of casting iron more efficiently. From his researches the coke smelting process for iron was born, and he moved to Coalbrookdale. Baptist Mills were renamed the

Bristol Brass Company and they continued to operate successfully.

Other works were opened at Keynsham, Chew Hill, Siston and Redbrook in Monmouth. In 1711 a copper refinery works was started near Bristol to supply the ore for the new processing works, though much imported ore was still used.

In 1719 a new works was opened in Cheadle which made sheet metal and ingots to be turned into the finished products elsewhere. Bristol in contrast was primarily a producer of drawn wire or finished battery.

Some of Cheadle's sheet metal or brass ore went to Birmingham, but the growth of this city's brass industry was handicapped by the distance both the ore and coals had to be brought. In 1740 a brass works was opened at Coleshill and from then on Birmingham had its own local supply of brass. This local supply stimulated the growth of the Birmingham manufacture of battery and with the opening of the canal to the Staffordshire coal fields in 1769 the growth of Birmingham received another major boost.

Over the next thirty years Birmingham became not only the centre of the brass industry in this country, but the largest in the world.

Throughout the eighteenth century the production process remained small scale. Most workshops employed only a few employees. The largest undertakings were naturally the mines and the workshops where the copper was turned into brass; the smallest were operated by craftsmen who made this brass into the finished products.

In spite of the vast expansion of the industry many were to find the going tough. The newspapers in the middle of the century were full of bankruptcies of brass and copper workers. But for every failure there was another man ready to try his luck. Most of them were under-capitalised and if they possessed the necessary technical skills, were often without business experience.

The expansion in brass and copper manufacturing can be illustrated by two sets of statistics. British copper mined rose from around 400 tons per annum in 1725 to over 2,000 tons per annum in 1760 and reached a peak around 1780 with over 5,000 tons. This peak was due to the great productivity of the new Anglesey mines. This massive production flooded the market and briefly drove copper prices down. Production was limited to about 3,000 tons per annum by the 1800s.

The second indicator of the growth of domestic production are the levels of finished goods imported into this country.

63 An eighteenth-century print showing brass and copper workers engaged in several tasks. The power is provided by a man turning a wheel (fig 3). A vessel is being turned to finish it (fig 2) and hammermen are at work (figs 1 & 6).

Between 1700-1704 an average of 227 tons of finished battery were brought in yet by the 1720s this had shrunk to 64·7 tons. After 1725 exports of battery began to exceed imports, and by 1770 only 7 tons of worked battery were disembarked, whereas exports amounted to 2,725 tons in an average year.

The growing standard of living and the expanding population led to a great increase in demand and the brass industry was also able to develop substantial markets overseas, especially in the North American Colonies and as barter for the slave trade to West Africa.

The following table shows the average level of exports for copper- and brass-worked products during the eighteenth century.

EXPORTS
WROUGHT COPPER AND BRASSWARE
10 year averages

Years	*Tons*
1700-09	92
1710-19	160
1720-29	230
1730-39	485
1740-49	846
1750-59	1243
1760-69	2251
1770-79	2725
1780-89	3131
1790-99	7228

Thus exports rose 79-fold in the eighteenth century. During the same period pewter exports only increased by $5\frac{1}{2}$-fold which illustrates dramatically the speed with which brass and copper products created a world market for themselves and led to the decline in pewter. The export figures do include all forms of production and are not exclusively domestic in purpose.

During the first half of the eighteenth century the methods used to make brass remained unchanged in this country and in Europe. Once the brass was made it was either turned into sheet metal using heavy trip hammers or sold as brass ingots to be cast. The two-part sand mould was universally used for larger objects by now. The use of patterns meant that an object could be cast several times and a degree of mass production was now possible. The making of these patterns was a very skilled task and there was a considerable trade in finished patterns. For example Horton and Jarvis of Birmingham were in 1775 offering for sale 'a sett of the neatest and newest patterns'.

When the casting was complete the item had to be cleaned off to remove excess metal. It was then burnished whilst held in a vice. Then the piece was finally polished by hand. Lathes were used in the second half of the eighteenth century for the speeding up of the finishing process. A polishing lathe was offered for sale in Birmingham in 1756, an engine lathe in 1763 for example. Such machinery was costly; a new engine lathe was worth up to 80 guineas.

After polishing was complete the piece was dipped in an acid bath and then it was often lacquered to prevent oxidisation.

In 1769, a process patented for stamping small objects out of sheet metal was taken up by Richard Forde of Birmingham who later used the process for larger products like warming pans, saucepans, ladles, basins and kettles. However, there is evidence that ten years earlier stamping had been in use for small objects. In 1757 stamps were offered for sale, one big enough 'to stamp buckles'.

A major change that was to revolutionise the brass making industry was ushered in in 1738 when William Chapman of Bristol took out a patent for the distillation of pure zinc. From this time on it was possible to use pure zinc ore rather than the crushed calamine zinc with all its impurities and complications. Chapman built the first zinc manufacturing plant in Bristol in 1743. Once the method of refining metallic zinc had been discovered it ought to have been possible to make brass by direct fusion, but the final step was not taken until 1781. Makers continued to use the old cementation process but replaced the calamine zinc with the metallic zinc. In the cementation method the temperature did not need to rise above 1000°F for the copper did not have to melt. The calamine was absorbed into the copper, fused to it while the copper was solid. It was a wasteful process with much loss of zinc. As the zinc was gradually absorbed into the copper the melting point of the copper-zinc alloy fell and at that state the copper may have melted. In the direct fusion process the copper was heated to above 1150°F and the zinc added to it. If just placed on the surface much would boil off at once, but by pushing the zinc below the liquid copper this loss could be contained and much higher proportions of zinc incorporated with the copper which, as it could be stirred, was more evenly mixed. The new process led to the abandonment of the old ways of brass making and eliminated the cause of the uneven quality of the brass. Without such a move the mass production which was to follow this and other changes would have been held back.

Though the role of Birmingham was very important brass was made in several other parts of the country throughout the eighteenth century. Bristol retained its secondary role and there was casting in Bridgewater, Chester, London and St Albans as well as in many small country towns where one or two craftsmen would have made things for the local populace.

Many of these local braziers also worked in other metals; it was also true that even in the major centres like Birmingham many men worked in more than one area of metal production. John Pidgeon of Digbeth Street and Edward Durnell of Bull Street (who in 1778 claimed to have the oldest established braziers shop in town) both made pewter as well as brass and copper ware.

Though most firms making brass objects did so on a small scale there was one exception. This was the great Birmingham Brass Company formed by Mathew Boulton and James Watt. From 1781 it was far and away ahead of all its rivals both in size and techniques.

The growth of brass manufacture, though spectacular was not without its setbacks. The war of 1793 had a considerable impact on the export trade, holding back the natural growth of trade.

The industrial revolution had already taken much of Britain in its grip by 1800. Factories using steam or water power were engaged in the production of textiles. Iron was being smelted in iron foundries in great quantities. There was a dramatic movement from the land to the factory, from the small villages and towns to the cities. Whereas in 1700 eight out of ten lived in the country, by 1900 four out of five were city or town dwellers. Development and change was everywhere, bringing with it abject poverty and apalling slum conditions as well as, for many, another chance in life as an alternative to nearly equally awful rural poverty.

The movement to the towns is highlighted when one finds that cities such as Manchester and Glasgow saw their population rise by two and a half times in the same period and Birmingham, Liverpool and Leeds by over twofold. Manchester with a population around 75,000-80,000 in 1800 had over 400,000 people by 1850. Over the same period the total population grew one and a half times.

Industrial production doubled between 1801 and 1831. Indeed the growth of the population, the drift to the cities and the vast growth of industrial production transformed the whole face of Britain within forty years. Yet if this phenomena of change was rapid in the first three decades it was nothing to the vast increases in production, the startling changes in techniques and the improvements in transport the next fifty years was to bring. In statistical terms a new scale for comparison is needed to appreciate the magnitude of the development within the economy. Industrial production, for example, which had risen twofold in the first thirty years of the century was to rise by nearly another sevenfold by 1913. Between 1800 and 1870 the production of coal rose twelvefold and in place of canals and their barges and roads and the cart, by 1870 more than 15,000 miles of railways were linking the industrial cities to the ports and the great cities with their insatiable demand for the products of the steam-powered factories.

Birmingham saw its share of this prosperity. In 1800 the total British production of copper was some 3,000 tons per annum yet by 1865 Birmingham alone used 20,000 tons a year, some imported, some from the new Cornish mines.

Even as early as 1802-3 Birmingham was rightly described as the most important brass producer in the world. A Scandinavian writer in 1802-3 wrote about the city 'which is famed on account of its factories and on account of its vast quantity of ornamental and metalwares which for thirty years have been directed from there all over the world'.

In spite of the vast changes in industry as a whole and not denying the substantial increase in production that occurred in brass making, the amazing feature of this period of great technological change is that in the brass industry the change was so small and so slow.

It would have been natural to assume that in brass making as

Firms engaged in various sections of brass industry in Birmingham
*Some firms appear more than once if they worked in more than a single area

1830
rest 9%
lamps and tubes 16%
wire and milling 6%
candlesticks 6%
plumbing 12%
foundary and stamping 51%

1865
plumbing 12%
lamps and tubes 25%
wire and milling 7%
candlesticks 2%
rest 12%
foundary and stamping 42%

with other industries such as iron, textiles and engineering, the workers would have been brought together in large factories, operating steam-powered machinery and adopting as their brothers in other crafts were, all the latest skills. The picture of what occurred in the brass industry in Birmingham is very different. Progress was slow. In the 1850s and '60s, for example, local commentators were still writing about the failure to adopt steam power as a means of improving production. Steam did not become really widespread in the brass industry until after 1865. Whereas in the eighteenth century most small Birmingham factories employed a handful of men and only a few as many as twenty or more, there was some increase in workshop size but nothing like the scale found in other industries. The numbers of people employed in Birmingham in the brass industry did rise from around 1700 in 1831 to over 8,000 by 1861, but it was not to reach its peak of 45,000 until 1913. The bulk of these men and women were still employed as late as 1870 in small units.

Just why brass makers in Birmingham were so slow to adopt steam power, the principles of the division of labour and factory methods is not clear.

The very success which attended the craft may have blinded masters to the advantages of the changes open to them. With production and demand rising fast they may not have felt any economic impulse for technological change. It may be that with individual skill so vital in the craft the great traditions of individuality helped to discourage change.

Linked with this increase both in employment and production was a steady increase in the number of firms working in brass or its allied trades. In 1800 it is estimated that perhaps fifty firms worked in the brass industry in Birmingham. By 1830 this had risen to 160 and by 1865 to 216.

The nature of the products worked also showed a considerable shift. More than half of the fifty or so firms operating in 1800 were founders or stamped out metal and the remaining number of firms were more or less equally divided amongst those operating in the plumbing area, candlestick makers, rolled brass or wire makers and other smaller trades. The pattern changed by 1830 with the appearance of many firms working in gas fittings, lamps and tubes and by 1865 the greatly expanded number of firms now included 25 per cent devoted basically to these new areas and the traditional field of candlestick making had slightly contracted in real numbers and relatively had lost considerably in importance. The changing pattern between 1830 and 1865 is illustrated in the diagrams on p. 103.

There were of course, those firms who did adopt new technology sooner than the majority and there were many important innovations during the nineteenth century. For example, in 1838 the making of seamless tubes was made possible following the work of Charles Green and this opened up the market for the manufacture of gas fittings more cheaply. Shortly after William Grice found a way to ornament these tubes using dies and thus led the way to the many decorated gas, electric and candle fittings based on arms made of tubes that were to be found in Victorian Britain.

All this production placed strains on the availability of copper from the Cornish mines and considerable quantities had to be imported. Old metal was still re-used and in 1865 it has been calculated that it accounted for 30 per cent of the copper ore.

A brass founder wrote in the eighteenth century that the practice of the Birmingham manufacturer '. . . was to keep within the warmth of his own forge'. Traditionally the makers made their goods, placed them in their own shops and sat back and waited for orders. This may have worked in the early years of the eighteenth century, but a more efficient way of bringing products to the attention of potential customers was needed. One way adopted by manufacturers was to produce pattern books. These pattern books throw a fascinating light on the kind of brassware being produced in Britain in the late eighteenth century. They show a great range of goods being marketed of which only a small proportion are household objects. They show too that though the manufacture of household items was still important in the nineteenth century the great advances in production were mostly in the industrial field. What in 1700-1750 was basically a domestic market had become, by 1900, industrial.

Chapter 10

What to look for in brass copper and bronze

Marks, makers and decoration

Very few brass, copper and bronze pieces carry any makers mark. As a consequence one of the most effective ways of dating is denied to students of base metals.

However, there are exceptions. A few early cooking pots or cauldrons have a merchants' mark, usually a simple device originally cut into the clay mould. Time has hidden where these makers worked, or who they were. Fine mortars were also often signed. Here we are more fortunate and we have been able to identify some of the makers.

In the north of England there are several mortars signed 'SS' and 'Ebor', the Latin for York. The Sellars family, including a Samuel, worked in York around 1680, and there was also another founder Samuel Smith at about this time.

In London, the famous Whitechapel foundry was run by Joseph Carter at the start of the seventeenth century and then by his son William *circa* 1615. Mortars are found with both their signatures. Thomas Bartlett who took over the Carters' works also marked mortars. There are many other makers of the seventeenth century whose names have been found on mortars and these include Henry Knight of Reading, *circa* 1618, John Martin of Worcester, *circa* 1681, Henry Bagley of Banbury, *circa* 1680, the Ashtons, Ralf and Luke of Wigan from 1700, Thomas Cheese of Bury St Edmunds, *circa* 1603-33 and John Palmer of Canterbury, the skillet maker, made several mortars around 1630. Near to where I live, the Neale family, father and son, worked throughout the 1630-85 period in Burford and there are several mortars signed Edward Neale either by father or son.

With skillets we will see later that the Palmers and John Fathers signed many of their products in the seventeenth century. In the eighteenth century Robert Bayley of Birmingham and Street of Bridgewater were prolific makers. Street was

for a time in partnership with another Bayley. The Street family appear to have been active between 1730 and 1810. Street in partnership with a Pike for example, advertised in the Exeter *Flying Post* in 1775 to sell 10,000 sets of money weights. Another active eighteenth-century maker was Rice of Bristol and Warner, also probably a west of England maker who was busy around 1800.

Many skillets are found signed Washborough and these are often erroneously attributed to the seventeenth century. Washborough worked on his own in Bristol between 1793 and 1826 and both before and after these dates in partnership with other makers. Most Washborough skillets are nineteenth century.

Surprisingly, few candlesticks have been marked by their makers. The following is a list of those I have found and where I have been able to trace their origins or period this is indicated:

I. Bayley	Birmingham	*circa* 1760
Barlow		*circa* 1800-20
'D' possibly Durley	Birmingham	*circa* 1770
George Grove	Birmingham	dead 1768
G.M.		mid-eighteenth century
E.K.		1780-1820
Joseph Wood		1735-60
Turner & Co.		*circa* 1750
William Lee	Birmingham	retired 1780
Lakin		*circa* 1740
Smith Carlisle		1760
W.S. with Crown		*circa* 1800-20

A substantial number of other firms are known to have made domestic brass in general and specialised lines as well, but it was not the general practice to mark their products until the late nineteenth century.

In spite of the absence of makers' marks there are words or phrases on metalware which can be of help in dating.

For example the word 'Patent' is an indication that the piece is no earlier than the mid eighteenth century. The use of a

Victorian registered number indicates an item made after 1884. The appearance of the words 'Trade Mark' means that the piece was made after 1862 and probably some time later. The origin of the object indicated by the word 'England' shows that it is after 1891 whilst the phrase 'Made in England' is twentieth century. The words 'Limited' or the letters 'Ltd' do not appear until after the Companies Act in 1862.

It became the practice for major stores and some larger makers to stamp on the base of their stocklines the pattern number of the object. The existence of such a stock number is an indication that the object was made in the last half of the nineteenth century or later.

Standard markings, that is those marks placed on objects by the weights and measures inspectors can help on occasions in dating things made for public use in the tavern or market place. Few pieces of brassware or bronze carry marks before the 1826 Imperial Standards. Thereafter the GRIV, WRIV, VR marks etc are all indicators of age. The chances are that anything with an ER or GR stamp being made prior to 1902 are not high, but it is possible that some Victorian items may have escaped marking in the early part of their working life.

Brass and copper did not receive the stamps of the authorities as easily as did pewter, and it was often the practice to add a small lead seal to a vessel and then place the capacity stamp upon that seal. The presence of such a seal, which has been defaced, is a strong indicator that someone wanted you to think that it was earlier than it is.

We will see that many items in copper, brass or bronze are decorated.

This can take many forms. Cast decoration is not uncommon and many patterns have also been raised on objects by either embossing on a form or under a machine while some patterns have been raised by hand. Punched designs are frequently found and fretted brassware was especially popular. There are many examples too, of the work of engravers both to decorate or to identify the owner of a piece.

Many early pieces of copperware were gilded and it was common too in Europe for some early copper to be treated similarly with silver. Some such work may have been undertaken over here, but most pieces with gilding or silvering are European.

The whole field of ormulu, the form of eighteenth-century gilding created in France and adopted in this country is outside the scope of this book. It is always necessary to look carefully at pieces which might at one time have been silver-plated whether in the traditional Sheffield form or more recently through electro-plate. Items once silver-plated have a diminished value and appeal to pieces made to stand in their own right unadorned.

Condition, cleaning and restoration

There is no doubt that the same rules ought to be applied to buying copper, brass and bronze as I have suggested for pewter. Look for the best-quality items that you can find and avoid as far as possible damaged or repaired pieces.

If you do have a piece that you want repaired the task is less difficult to get done than with pewter for there are more metalsmiths about than pewterers these days. Most towns have someone capable of brazing brass and the problem of the low melting point so important with pewter is less likely to appear with copper alloys.

Simple repairs can be made with a silver or lead solder which if well done can almost be invisible. More professional repairs, actually brazing the piece, are a little more dangerous as the temperature has to be lifted to a point close to the melting point of the original materials. It must be realised too that heating brass or bronze changes the colour of the metal and that it will normally have to be repolished.

Should there be a piece to be replaced it is necessary to make a judgement as to the nature of the alloy originally used for otherwise the repair will stand out from the original only too clearly.

The colour of a piece may give you some idea of its contents. Under about 30 per cent of zinc, the colour will be golden, getting stronger or more red as the proportion of zinc falls. Over 50 per cent zinc gives a whitish colour while naturally, pieces with little zinc at all will be highly copper coloured.

Copper, brass and bronze do all oxidise slowly, but this rarely forms the same thick coat as is found with pewter. The eruptions found in pewter, once called tin pest, are also not matched in these copper alloys.

The debate regarding favoured colour as a consequence hardly exists. Most people prefer their brass or copper cleaned and polished. There are a few connoisseurs, especially in Europe who look for a dark even patina of oxide, but most collectors accept pieces far more polished than they would in pewter. Bronze by contrast, is often sought in its original dark condition and pieces which have been cleaned and buffed are less prized.

There is a danger too in cleaning bronze that has been used

in the fire over long periods. The original imperfect mixture of the alloys may have allowed some of the trace elements and hardeners to be burnt out of the metal and if this pocked surface is now cleaned small pits and indentations may appear.

One of the objections that some people have to brass and copper is that it does need regular cleaning. It very quickly shows signs of oxiding, especially if handled. The use of any spirit-based cleaner will quickly restore the piece to its original colour unless the oxide is very old and deep when it may have to be dipped in a caustic substance and rebuffed. But this should always be done professionally and most carefully so as not to damage the piece or take away any signs of age and wear.

How to date copper, brass and bronze

In Europe there was considerable interest in brass and bronze and copies abound. There were copies of Roman and Greek bronzes being made in the sixteenth century. In the nineteenth century the interest in the Gothic style was considerable. Amongst the items most copied are Dutch dated mortars, Italian cooking pots, many of them dated about 1610 and German alms dishes. In this country the interest in brass is very recent and until the last fifteen years or so few items had much value. Hence, whilst they have been extensively reproduced the number of deliberate fakes is very small indeed.

You are up against therefore, not the skilled faker trying to fool you with his skill, but a modern copy. The enemy is ignorance and gullibility fathered by greed. The task is basic-ally to separate modern copies from the original not to try and distinguish a finely crafted fake. But do remember that your grandparents were buying brass objects for use from some of the major stores as late as 1910, similar in style to many of the Georgian pieces that we will examine. Throughout the 1920s and '30s there were several firms who specialised in casting and making up direct copies of earlier pieces and also pieces which ape the style of the old, but which were never actually made historically. Extracts from some of these catalogues are illustra-ted to show the kinds of things that were being reproduced. Not all dealers can tell the old from the new; and as someone once suggested to me some will never be able to do so whilst there is a financial advantage in ignorance. A few shady characters may be actively ageing modern reproductions, acid etching the surface, putting on artificial wear with knife and hammer, turning a rough casting off to resemble the old finish, etc.

But if you remember that up to the middle of the nineteenth

century all copper and brass was made by hand, each piece individually finished to a high quality, and that domestic objects were made to be used, then many of the problems will fall away.

The first thing to look at, I would suggest, is purpose; what was the object made to do. This will often tell us something about the period in which it may have been made. This is not always so as something may have remained in use over very long periods, but it is surprising how often the reason why a piece was made can help to date it for us.

We know for example that flat-bottomed cooking vessels were seldom used before the late seventeenth century. And at the most obvious level you are not likely to find a Tudor gas light nor a Victorian acquamanile!

The style in which a thing is made may also help to date it. Compare the piece with illustrations in general and specialised studies. Identify if you can the kind of style that is closest to that of the piece you wish to identify. This will probably give you a further indication of its possible age, though it is always necessary to remember that some styles lasted over many years.

The alloys of which it is made would, if you could have the article analysed, add some further information, but this is normally not possible. If you think, however, that the proportion of zinc is likely to be above 30 per cent then you have a watershed (around 1770 when the use of mineral zinc became more widespread) after which it is likely to have been made. The whiter the colour the less golden the brass, the higher the zinc. The existence of trace elements would also be a sign that the piece was made prior to the ability to refine copper effectively for pure copper was seldom used prior to the mid nineteenth century.

Much more can be learnt by looking carefully at how the thing was made. Has it been cast or was it raised from sheet metal by hammering?

If cast, does it appear to have been a one off production of sand or clay moulds, often a little crude and irregular, or does it clearly bear the signs of a very even highly accurate mould? If it is made from sheet metal, how thick is the sheet? Is it rather thicker than most modern brass and is it a little uneven? If so it may have been hammered out by trip hammers or by a hammerman rather than rolled out in a rolling mill.

Look at any joins in the piece. Are there seams and what form do they take? Dovetailing was the traditional way of making joins. The dovetails were carefully cut, the two pieces

65 Not only were many objects raised from sheets of metal by hammering but nearly all were finished by this technique. Here is an illustration of an eighteenth-century bowl, showing the hammermarks where the bowl was shaped. The turning on the body can also be clearly seen.

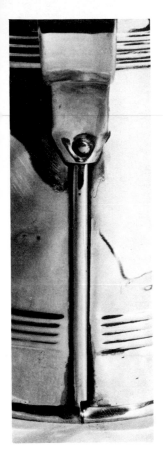

66 The overlap seam, a sign of nineteenth-century manufacture. The sheets of metal are bent over each other and hammered or pressed into position.

67 *Opposite:* A dovetailed seam. The most frequently used method before the advent, in the nineteenth century, of machinery to make overlap seams.

put together and hammered to complete the waterproof joint. Dovetailing was in use up to 1900 but was generally out of fashion by the mid nineteenth century.

The other popular seam was the overlap. That is a small piece of the metal was bent back to form a narrow flange and this was locked into a similar flange on the other piece to be joined, the two interlocking flanges then being hammered out to make the joint permanent. Such a form of seaming indicates a nineteenth century date.

Another method used was to solder the joint and this method was used in the seventeenth century, but not where any great pressure was to be brought to bear or where the temperatures involved in the life of the piece were going to be high. A simple soldered seam is an indicator of a modern finish.

Other indicators are the thickness of the metal in castings. The use of patterns, sand moulds or metal moulds produce a thinner casting than the earlier clay mould would have done.

Handles too can give further help. If they are hollow cast are they seamed on one side? If so they can be of any age, but if seamless they must be nineteenth century. Solid handles are an indication that a piece is prior to 1700.

Look at the way the piece has been finished off after manufacture.

The bases of flagons, tankards and the like were all carefully cleaned off and then turned on a wheel to give a fine even finish. An eighteenth-century maker would in no way have thought of sending out something with the marks of the sand casting still upon it than the modern maker of a Rolls Royce car would countenance selling it unpainted. The presence of a surface still rough from the casting is almost without exception a sign that the piece is not old.

Where it was possible, for example on all round based objects, the bases were carefully polished on a lathe and there will be signs of this fine turning. Years of use and care will have smoothed out the ridges. If the turning is still rough to touch and consists of deep ridges well spaced out it may well be of recent origin.

The three main techniques for joining parts together where seaming was not appropriate are casting in the mould, soldering and riveting.

The term cast joints is misleading for there is no joint at all, the pieces being cast as one within the original mould. This technique was mostly used in bronze pieces where the stresses would be very heavy such as skillets, cooking pots and mortars. The soldering of parts is a sign of nineteenth-century

1302

1303

1297

1308

1305

1299
LARGE

1307

1306

1309

1311

1310

1312

1286
LARGE

1299
MEDIUM

1313

68 A page from a 1920s catalogue of reproduction brass. Most jardinières that you will see are from this period.

construction and should be suspect if found on a piece designed to carry considerable stresses. The most effective way of joining two parts is to rivet them together; early rivets were thick and hammered on both sides to complete the joint. Thin rivets, often only visible from one side, are a sign of later construction, perhaps post-1860.

Screw threads are another way of dating metalware. When they are present they should be examined to see whether they have been hand cut or machine made. Hand cut threads are always further apart, more uneven and the ridges are usually

69 A group of reproduction candlesticks from the same catalogue.

deeper. The presence of modern screws is a sure sign of recent manufacture, unless they are clearly replacements. In eighteenth-century and some earlier candlesticks there were threads cut onto the stems. The use of a separate screw to join the two parts of the candlestick is a sign of nineteenth-century origin.

The last criteria for judging age to be examined is 'wear'. Does the item show sufficient evidence of age to support the kind of date that the other tests have suggested? Is the wear in those parts which naturally carry the most stress? Basically this is a matter of common sense; plates should have knife scratches, bowls, dents and so on. The eye can tell a lot, but let the fingers do the talking as well. Run your hands over the piece; are there sharp edges? If there are these should either have been taken off when made or worn down by use. In the end it's a simple question that you have to ask yourself? Is there the kind of evidence of hard uncaring use that you would expect to see. Loving care came with the first collector to own the item and if you doubt that and have romantic ideas of how your forefather's looked after their possessions look at some of the baking tins and other kitchen utensils in your own kitchen and you will see what I mean!

One area which can present difficulties is where an original part has been married to an original part of another object. Good period metalware is sometimes found with a recently made replacement. Charles II trumpet-based candlesticks seem particularly vulnerable to this treatment because of their value. There are also marriages to alter the purpose of a piece. Some fine Stuart warming pan lids have, for example, recently been converted into wall sconces by adding candle-holders to them. Always check that the colours of a piece made in more than one part are the same, that they carry the same basic degree of wear and that they fit properly together.

The technique for dating all these objects, therefore, involves looking at their purpose, construction, style and wear. Where all tell the same story a clear date will probably emerge; where there is conflict then there are grounds for further examination and consideration.

A couple of examples may help to illustrate how this can work out in practice.

Take the curfew illustrated on plate 129. From the section on keeping warm (Chapter 13) we have learnt that curfews gradually went out of popularity in the eighteenth century. In style you would find if you were able to examine others in museums and reference books, that it is similar to examples from around 1680-1720. It was made by carefully riveting hand raised sheets of latten to each other and as you can see the surface shows plenty of evidence of wear including the tops of the slight embossing being polished out. All of the factors therefore tell the same basic story that the curfew is probably around 1700.

Let us now look at a Georgian style candlestick. We can learn nothing much from its purpose, but style will tell us a little more.

70 *Above:* Most objects in brass and copper were carefully completed by turning. Bases were cleaned off and turned. Here is an illustration of an eighteenth-century square-based candlestick base showing the turning. Even where the base could not be turned (in the corners) it has been cleaned off with chisels.

71 *Right:* The base of a reproduction candlestick showing its uneven unfinished nature. The original sand-casting marks can be clearly seen.

From its square base you would suppose that it must date from after 1760 and the Corinthian stem suggests also a date of about 1780.

The method of construction confirms that it has been cast and that as there is a pusher in the base it is likely to have been hollow cast. This strengthens our hypothesis that it is around 1760.

We now look at the way it has been finished, its wear and general appearance. By turning up the candlestick we find that it has not been turned off, that there are, under a glass, some remnants of the metal deposited in the mould and not completely cleaned off. Compare the base with that of the other candlestick shown here.

By running our fingers over the edges of the base and candle holder we may be able to feel a certain sharpness. The surface is smoothly buffed with few signs of wear and tear. There is very little damage at any point. So whilst the method of construction and style suggested an eighteenth-century date this we must now revise as it does not have sufficient wear nor is it well enough finished for that period. It may be nineteenth century or more recent, but it is not likely to be Georgian.

Where the bases are square they could be well finished off with chisels, and whatever roughness was left will probably have been worn away by rubbing and cleaning over the candlesticks' life.

In addition to re-turning the bases of candlesticks some sticks were also aged on the base by hammering to add a false impression of wear.

72 Sixteenth-century brass alms dish. The scene is of St George and the Dragon. From either Dinant or Nuremberg such dishes were on display in wealthy homes. None were made in this country but many were imported for use here.

73 A fine medieval jug. Its bronze-like colour disguises its high copper content. *c.* 1450. Private collection.

Continental forms: brass and copper
 1 Dutch kettle
 2 German kettle
 3 Dutch tankard
 4 North European ewer
 5 German/Dutch jug
 6 German coffee pot
 7 Dutch coffee pot
 8 Dutch/German coffee pot
 9 German ewer
10 German coffee pot

117

74 *Left:* Decorated seventeenth-century lead bronze mortar. Private collection.

75 *Below:* A set of three brass tavern mugs from the late nineteenth century. Mostly used in public houses some will have been domestic.

76 *Opposite:* Fine late Victorian tea urn with gadrooned body. Earlier examples are mostly somewhat plainer in style.

77 *Pages 120-21:* An array of copper and brass pans such as would have been used in a great house, *c.* 1800-20. Royal Pavilion, Brighton.

78 *Above:* Brass and copper ladles, skimmers and serving spoons. All eighteenth century. Some with iron handles, others in brass.

79 *Left:* Copper kettles, saucepans and a food warmer from the Prince Regent's Kitchen. Royal Pavilion, Brighton.

80 *Opposite:* An eighteenth-century fireplace. The saucepans and kettle are probably nineteenth century but give an excellent impression of how a working kitchen's fireplace might have looked *c.*1800. Cambridge and County Folk Museum.

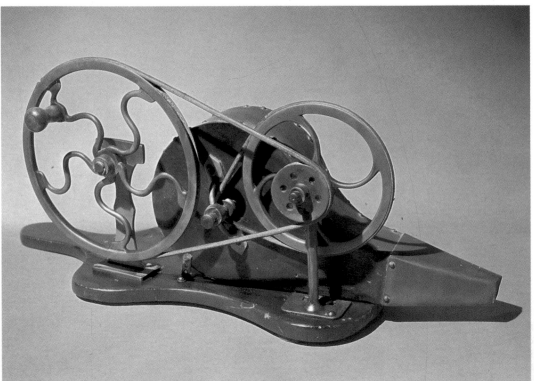

81 *Opposite:* A display of copper jelly moulds from the Royal Pavilion.

82 *Opposite below:* A pair of 'Irish Peat' bellows. These were used with all types of fires and many were made in Great Britain as well as Ireland. Collection of the Curator of Horsham Museum.

European metalware

There is no easy way to tell British from European base metalware. So few pieces are marked that it is necessary to learn the styles involved before the differences are apparent.

This becomes more and more possible in the seventeenth century and easier thereafter as the similarities in style gradually disappear. Judgements are made by experts about the origin of most medieval objects, but few readers will be faced by these problems. With the establishment of the British brass industry the styles popular in Europe and Britain did begin to take different routes.

On the whole, European brass ware and copper work is rather more elaborate. Spouts are more common and are larger, embossing is more pronounced, knops larger and lids bigger, handles are more decorative, feet more often seen.

But all these hints may just serve to confuse as there are elaborate, highly decorative British products! You will probably need to consult specialist books on those aspects of the industry that appeal to you most to learn about the Continental forms. Illustrated on p. 116 are some of the more important Continental shapes.

83 A typical coffee pot in copper, a form seldom found in this country but popular in Europe during the early nineteenth century.

125

Chapter 11

Copper brass and bronze in cooking

Because of their comparatively high melting points these alloys were ideal for cooking. Their only rivals until modern times were pottery, which was easy to break, and iron, which was difficult to cast before the early eighteenth century and liable to fracture.

Until the eighteenth century cooking was done over an open fire and this method survived in rural areas into the last century. Two principal forms of cooking utensils were used. The larger, used suspended over the flames or stood in the fire, the smaller with a handle and feet placed only in the flames.

These early pots were basically of a bronze alloy, but by the late seventeenth century brass was increasingly used for cooking utensils.

Except for the low temperature bread ovens, most cooking was done over the open fire. When there was meat to roast it was suspended on a spit before the fire and to help it to roast evenly the spits were turned either by hand, clockwork or even by animals.

The growing use of coal, especially in the towns, whose nearby countryside was denuded of timber by the late seventeenth century, led to grates replacing the andirons (these were metal stands used for supporting burning wood on the hearth). Gradually hobs were positioned by the fire and used for cooking. Out of these hobs in turn ovens were created so that by the late eighteenth century most town dwellers will have had a hob and oven. By the middle of the nineteenth century kitchen ranges were popular in large houses. Thereafter gas and then electricity were adopted for cooking though this development had less significance on cooking-pot design than the first great change from the open fire to the hob.

Every family needed hot water and the fire was the only means to provide this. A large pot was kept on the fire throughout the day and often overnight. These vessels were called 'kettles'. Many early kettles were flat-bottomed containers made of copper beaten into shape and riveted together.

84 *Right:* Fifteenth century bronze cooking pot with small mouth and tall feet. Victoria & Albert Museum, London.

85 *Far right:* A cooking pot from around 1600 with wide mouth and iron handle.

Other kettles had the more common rounded base and were made from bronze.

The cooking pot was used for cooking most food, especially the potages, porridge, gruels and stews. Roast meat would have been uncommon except in the great houses, and the bulk of a family's food was prepared in the rounded crock or cauldron suspended over the fire.

These cooking vessels were in use up to the seventeenth century and changed little in form. They were made all over Europe as well as this country and many pots were imported.

The earliest cooking pots were very rounded with small openings, but gradually the mouth became larger and the form less rounded. There are many local variations. By the sixteenth century the rims of cooking pots are larger than before and more flared.

Most, but not all of these cauldrons had three feet so that in addition to being suspended by their small handles, they could be stood directly in the fire. The regular contact with heat has meant that in most pots the feet are partly burnt away. In a few cases the pots will not stand on their legs, but wobble about in a most unseemly manner on their bottoms.

These pots came in many sizes, from the largest for hot water to small pots for sauces. In great houses many cooking pots will have been available for use; while in the poorest homes perhaps just one would have fulfilled all the family's needs. Very large quantities of these cauldrons must have been made and they have survived in some quantity. It is not easy to say with confidence whether any particular vessel was made in this country or in Europe as so many were imported and styles are very similar.

The other main group of early cooking utensils are the skillets or posnets. These smaller cooking vessels have three feet and a long handle at one side. Early posnets had the same rounded form as the cauldrons or crocks, but by the early seventeenth century the body is being made with straight sides slightly tapering outwards. About this time makers began to cast their names or to add suitable inscriptions on the handles. Most of these inscriptions had a political or religious basis; 'C you be Loyall to his Magister', 'Honour thy King', 'Pity the Poore', 'Love thy God' and the like are amongst the more popular exhortations.

There are a number of makers who signed their skillets, including the father and son partnership of John and Thomas Palmer of Canterbury (John *circa* 1635, Thomas 1660-80), and John Fathers/Feathers, presumed to be a west of England maker from around 1680. In the eighteenth century the Street family of Bridgewater were prolific makers. Skillets were still being made as late as 1830.

Some of the early skillets had finely cast feet on the bottom of the legs in the shape of an animal's hoof. As with cauldrons many of these feet and legs have been partly burnt away through use. You will find that skillets often lean slightly forwards having one foot, that most frequently in the fire, shorter than the other two.

Early skillets had a strap-like support beneath the handle reinforcing the joint. This strap is rather like the handles on cauldrons. By the eighteenth century this has been replaced by a solid stepped support. Skillets marked 1, 2 or 3 are usually post-imperial and the numbering indicated the capacity in pints.

Few cooking pots have a makers' mark other than a symbol scratched into the outer clay mould and it is not possible therefore, to identify cauldron makers. Dated cauldrons are also uncommon and even with skillets few bear dates prior to

1660. A dated pot before 1600 will be rare.

The move from cooking over the fire to using a hob which started in the seventeenth century, saw the greater use of flat-bottomed cooking vessels. The first to be popular was the frying pan. These were in service in the late seventeenth century. Frying pans up to perhaps 1800 had long handles, often in iron. They were slightly deeper than the pans we use today and considerably larger. The handle is joined to the body by heavy rivets, the pans raised from latten sheet by hammering.

During the eighteenth century saucepans with flat bottoms, deeper bowls and long handles began to be used. Gradually the handles of both frying pans and saucepans became shorter as the significance of the change from open cooking to using a hob became clear.

It is important to remember that all saucepans of this period were hand made, each individually raised from sheets of copper or latten. Joints when they existed were dovetailed. These sheet metal cooking utensils were heavy and thick. To our eyes they are crude and only in basic outline similar to what we now use.

Few of these saucepans or frying pans have lasted. They were heavily used and then traded in for new ones when no longer serviceable.

In the nineteenth century the sides of the saucepans become straighter and the handles are now always short. Later in the century a more rounded style again appears. A glance at the Army and Navy Stores catalogue for 1909 will show that many such saucepans were still being made and marketed. The basic difference between the products of the Regency days and those of the last decades of the nineteenth century is that the vessels

87 A mid-nineteenth-century saucepan and flat lid, both with iron handles.

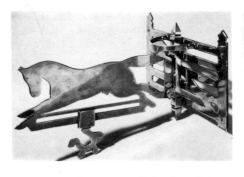 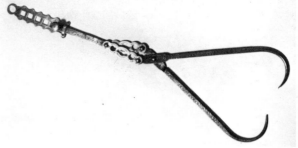

are now no longer made by hand, but either cast or stamped out from sheet. The unevenness of manufacture has given way to a conformity. Many Victorian and Edwardian saucepans had lids. The early form was a flattish disk which rested on top, the lid having its own separate iron or copper alloy handle. Later the lids were rounded and had a small strap handle on the top. After the 1870s many utensils were stamped either with a makers' mark or a patent number, but sometimes these have been filed off to give the pot an earlier appearance.

When you start looking about you at frying pans and saucepans on the market you will naturally see many more from the Edwardian days than you will genuine Georgian examples. A fine display of Regency cooking equipment is shown in the kitchen of the Royal Pavilion in Brighton.

One variety of cooking pan found in the nineteenth century was used mainly for jams or preserves. These jam pans have a flat base, usually dovetailed into the sides, and are well made of a heavy metal. Mostly made in brass the earlier examples have swing handles, but after the 1850s the handles are usually fixed in place.

Whilst most cooking was done over the open fire the pots had to be suspended above the flames by some device. Cranes or pot hooks were generally used. Cranes were much as their name implies. An arm set at right angles to the back of the chimney which could be raised or lowered by using ratchets. Most cranes are made in iron. There are however, a number of variations including some with a hook, moved up and down a straight bar on ratchets. There were also hooks, usually used in sets made of different sizes so that by selecting which to use the height of the pot above the flames could be correctly judged. Many of these were made in brass or copper.

Prior to the use of ovens, roasting was done on a spit. There were many varieties mostly made in iron, but a few decorated in brass or copper were made. The simplest form would have been a large iron spit, stood before the fire, which was turned

88 *Left:* A nineteenth-century brass crane for suspending pots and pans over the fire.

89 *Above:* A steel and brass meat hook c. 1700. The weight of the meat in the pincers kept them closed and the height could be adjusted by regulating the ratchets at the top.

90 A bottle Jack or clockwork spit. Nineteenth century. Brighton Museum.

by a handle. The most complicated were the clockwork spits of the eighteenth century. The earliest made by clockmakers were large and heavy. Later simple 'bottle' shaped spits were popular with a clockwork mechanism inside. These are usually made in brass and are called 'bottle jacks'.

Many other metal tools were to be found in use in the kitchen. Cutting tools were normally made in steel or iron, but spoons, ladles and skimmers were also in frequent use and many were in brass and occasionally copper. Prior to 1700 most were raised from sheet metal. Some handles are riveted onto the bowl; others are integral with it. In the eighteenth century iron handles were frequently used, but after 1850 'all brass' spoons were again produced. These have been extensively copied. There are some very decorative brass skimmers. These were called 'scummers' in the seventeenth century and were used to separate the butter from the butter milk, cream from the skimmed milk, fats from stews, etc. Early skimmers were simply flattened ladles with crude holes driven through the bowl. Most are made in brass. Later, iron handles were favoured and the holes in the brass more evenly punched. Very decorative shaped skimmers, made all in brass, are nineteenth century. The likelihood is that the more decorative they are the later they will be.

Colanders and straining dishes were to be found in many eighteenth-century homes; some in slipware or salt glazed pottery, a few in sheet or cast brass.

Pies have always been a popular form of food, hence 'simple Simon and the Pie man' and other nursery rhymes. From the late eighteenth century through the nineteenth, pastry wheels were used to add decoration to the pie crust. Early wheels or 'jiggers' sometimes have a spoon at one end. All the eighteenth-century examples appear to have been made wholly in brass. Wooden or bone handles were sometimes used in the nineteenth century and some of the later jiggers have three or even four different wheels or cutters.

The housewife of yesterday had no recourse to a mincer or blender. These tasks were performed with a pestle and mortar. The meat for the stew would have been pounded, herbs and spices ground and even medicines prepared, using the family mortar. Most seventeenth-century English mortars are made of a lead-bronze though for some of the specially commissioned mortars a lead-free alloy was used.

Most of the mortars made before the second half of the seventeenth century have either two or four lugs or handles. These lugs made it easier to hold and use the mortar.

131

During the seventeenth century many mortars were made without lugs. Though many sizes are found, the average size for a mortar was about four inches high.

Most seventeenth-century mortars are decorated. The principle emblems used have a political or religious meaning. There are mortars in honour of King Charles I with his portrait, death mask or coat of arms. There are a few of the Commonwealth period with the arms of Scotland, England and Ireland. Religious symbols used include the fleur-de-lys, symbolising both the holy trinity and purity, the gryffin with a key for the keys to the kingdom of heaven, the deer representing the hart in the field or Christ, etc.

Some mortars have a temporal decoration for example, those bearing City Arms or decorated with swags of flowers or owners, makers' names or initials. During the seventeenth century mortar shapes started to become less rounded. Mortars were still widely used into the nineteenth century, but after about 1750 they became plain and many were made in iron.

Pounded meats and grains were popular foods for our forefathers and in the Middle Ages they were known as 'mortrews'; an indication of the importance of the mortar and pestle to the cook of those times.

With the popularity of the 'cook book' in the late seventeenth and eighteenth century and more formal cooking, the need for measured quantities increased. Most early weights had been made for the market or fair. By Victorian times sets of weights were being made for domestic use. Several styles were made, the most popular of these are in the earlier waisted form. An average set would run from a seven-pound weight down to a weight of a quarter of an ounce. Nearly all of them had their weight engraved upon them or carried a lead stamp with a

91 *Left:* A fine lead bronze mortar by William Carter of the Whitechapel Foundry in London dated 1615. Later seventeenth-century mortars are usually straighter and more flared. Victoria & Albert Museum, London.

92 *Above:* A set of brass weights from the 7 lb down, for use in kitchen or shop. Victorian and therefore post-imperial measures.

confirmation of weight from the weights and measures officer. These check marks often help to date a set. Later sets of weights in the disk form are still often found, but not yet much collected.

To most people in the early days getting enough food to sustain life was a problem, especially in winter, but for the favoured few, food could be a pleasure as well as a necessity. Elaborate medieval banquets are recorded with much emphasis placed on display. A feature of these banquets were the sugared confections made in the shapes of birds and beasts.

In the eighteenth century the table was decorated with castles, boats, swans and elaborate designs made from spun sugar or cast in moulds. The making of desserts like jellies and custards in different shapes developed from these early decorations and were very popular in the nineteenth century.

Most jelly-moulds are made in copper, tinned inside. Moulds of the Regency period are likely to be larger than the later ones. They are made in a heavier metal and many are seamed. By the late Victorian times moulds were smaller, often stamped out of sheet and with a stock or pattern number on the base or side, a clear indicator on a piece of late construction. They were made in many hundreds of shapes and sizes mostly in the shapes of birds, flowers or fruit. The first Duke of Wellington possessed over 500 in his kitchen and many of them are now on display in the Royal Pavilion in Brighton.

In the medieval times, water was brought to the table in fine bronze containers known as aquamaniles. Many of them cast in elaborate shapes. Few if any of them are likely to have been made in this country. The simpler water or wine jug however was also used. The earliest cast in clay moulds with heavy mould lines. Those with a high copper content probably date back to the 1400s. During the following 200 years pewter largely replaced bronze at the table, but in the eighteenth century copper and brass jugs were again widespread.

The most popular form is bulbous, usually spouted. They were made of sheet metal, seamed with dovetails, up the body behind the handle. The eighteenth-century jugs are made in heavy metal, in the nineteenth century thinner sheet metal was used. The straight-sided jug was probably first made around 1780-1800. Both of these types normally have hollow cast handles.

In Scotland two other shapes were popular in the nineteenth century. One of baluster form, mostly made in copper, occasionally in brass, these are found in the imperial measure from the gill upwards and many will have been used in public

93 A quart copper jug with hollow handle c. 1800. The body was raised by hammering and the marks can still be seen.

94 Copper harvester measure. These measures were made in both brass and copper throughout the nineteenth century. Mostly for use in markets and shops a few will have been used in the home. Check the lead capacity seal as it may help to date the measure.

95 Two Scottish measures. The baluster style on the left is often in copper. That on the right the rarer thistle style usually in brass. Both are post-imperial.

houses. The smaller sizes are lidless, but from the quart upwards they have slightly domed lids.

The other Scottish type is thistle-shaped, again made in both copper and brass. They have hollow handles and the bases underneath are slightly concave and have been soldered into position; another indicator of their nineteenth century origin. Brass tappit hens are occasionally offered for sale, but I have yet to see an example which I have thought to have been made before the end of the nineteenth century.

The importance of ale, beer and wine gradually declined with the introduction of tea and coffee to the national diet.

Coffee which first appeared in Europe around 1580 reached these shores in 1650. It never attained the importance of tea over here and at first was mostly drunk by gentlemen in coffee shops. The first to be opened, it is claimed, was in Oxford.

The earliest coffee pots are tapering in form with a tall rounded domed lid which has a small knop. They have a long pouring spout set at right angles to a straight wooden handle. Later a strap handle replaces the wooden grip and the handle is placed opposite the spout. The tapering body then gives way to a more rounded pear-shape and later in the eighteenth century the body takes on a concave form and the straight wooden handle opposite the spout reappears. Most coffee pots made after the 1840s are in copper and have been tinned.

Chocolate pots are often very similar in shape to the coffee pot, but have a small hole in the lid through which the sticky liquid could be stirred. In the mid to late nineteenth century the handles of both coffee and chocolate pots were often bound with raffia or cane to make them heat resistant. The concave form of pot was still being made in the 1900s.

Tea reached Europe, via Portugal and Holland, in the seventeenth century. The first public tea sale was held in 1657 and at the start it was a very costly commodity and limited to the homes of the rich. In the 1660s tea cost £3.50p a pound, a year's wages for a maid. By 1700 it was still over £1 a pound and though its price was to fall in the next half-century, in the 1760s you would have had to pay 50p a pound when meat was under $1\frac{1}{2}$p per pound.

In spite of this high price the demand for tea rose dramatically and it had adherents at all levels of society. Boswell wrote of it, 'I am so fond of tea that I could write a whole dissertation on its virtues'.

In the well-to-do home it was drunk with lemon or sugar and a high-quality tea could be afforded. In the working-man's home it was taken with brown sugar and was a weak brew from inferior leaf. Whatever its cost or quality it had replaced beer as the national drink by 1800.

At first tea was drunk from porcelain tea bowls and poured from tea pots made in the Chinese style. Around 1700 silver was used to make tea pots and there were also a few pots made in pewter. Tea pots in brass or copper are rare from all periods as silver, plate, pottery and porcelain seem to have been preferred.

Of the few made in brass or copper the earliest form is bullet-shaped and later they were made in the typically Georgian and Victorian styles. But look out for coffee or tea pots that were at one time silver-plated.

96 Two coffee pots; both forms found in copper and brass. That on the left is c. 1800; the example on the right from the early nineteenth century.

Tea urns were made in both copper and brass. The straight-sided and baluster-shaped urns of the eighteenth century are mostly Dutch imports but from 1800 onwards many urns were made here.

Some stand on a pedestal base and have round knopped lids. A few have spirit lamps beneath for heating the water. They all have small taps in the base. Many tea urns or 'samovars' as they are called were made in silver plate. Urns with pottery finials or taps are likely to be Edwardian in period.

Tea kettles developed parallel with the habit of tea drinking. There are many hundreds of designs in copper or brass. Kettles were made in a number of sizes from a pint up to a monster of two gallons or more. They come square, round or oval. As with all domestic metalware the early kettles are made from heavy duty sheet dovetailed together; later kettles from thin sheet evenly rolled. Kettles with rounded movable handles tend to be early nineteenth century, those with fixed handles later. Handles made of other materials indicate a late-nineteenth-century origin.

Kettles in copper and brass were made in vast quantities for export as well as for the home market. Recently copper kettles sent to North Africa in the late nineteenth century have been brought back here and at the same time modern copper kettles from the Middle East have been imported in quantity to fill the demand for these attractive pieces, so pleasing when placed by the fireside.

Kettles were made to withstand plenty of hard wear and if they have been around they should show signs of heavy use, especially on the base.

97 A group of kettles. Usually in copper but brass examples do occur and are much valued. The two kettles on the left have straight rounded handles and are mid nineteenth century. The example on the right is slightly earlier.

98 A seventeenth-century apostle spoon in brass; the round bowl dates it to be about 1650.

Brass and copper were also used at table. A few brass-handled steel knives are known, but forks were seldom made in brass or bronze and those that do appear are French or Italian. Spoons in latten or brass, on the other hand, were numerous and spoons with an interesting variety of knops can be found. Examples from as early as the 1300s can still be bought; many of the early examples will have been made in Europe and imported, but their use in Britain is authenticated.

Most of the knops found in pewter are duplicated in latten. The later-eighteenth-century examples are not common and in the nineteenth century whilst copper spoons were made they were mostly plated though by now this plate may have worn away.

Latten spoons are not found quite as frequently as pewter spoons, perhaps in the ratio of 6 to 5. About 40 per cent of all latten spoons have seal-top finials. Apostle spoons make up about another 20 per cent, although many of these are Continental. The tryfid, slip top, horses hoof and puritan knopped spoons account in total for about 15 per cent. None of the other knops appear on more than one spoon in a hundred.

Salts in brass are not common even in the eighteenth century. The few that there are are mostly in cup salt form or on a short stem.

Peppers, sanders, sugar and spice sifters are less rare though seventeenth-century examples are hard to find. Most of those that are still around are in the baluster or urn shape. The straight-sided sifter with strap handle was used for spices or for flour.

There are far fewer brass or copper plates and dishes than are found made in pewter. Those plates that do exist are mostly in copper, made with a single-reeded rim. Dishes are even rarer though there are a few examples. Be careful when buying oval or round copper dishes to ensure that they were not once silver-plated.

A very few brass or copper porringers from the 1700s have survived, they are similar in shape to those in pewter, but beware of small two-eared brass porringers with a cast Tudor rose in the base; these are modern and made in Holland.

Plate warmers, stands on which pewter or china plates would be kept warm for use at the table, are often found in brass. The most popular form is the four-legged 'cat' in which the plates rest on the four arms which cross to form the feet beneath. Less common is the style with round base and uprights into which the plates are put one on top of the other.

Brass or copper tankards and flagons are rare. There are a

99 Copper ale muller. This form is known as the 'boot'. The other typical shape was just tapering rather like a funnel with closed end. Ale and other drinks were often taken hot and spiced. Nineteenth century.

few fine early-eighteenth-century examples, in most Georgian styles. Concave-sided copper tankards were common in the second half of the nineteenth century. Again often plated, most were for use in taverns which is also where most of the brass and bell-metal bellied and straight-sided tankards were used. These styles are all similar to the pewter mugs from which they are derived.

There were also some goblets made in brass in the late nineteenth century, with deep bowls and short stems they were made of good heavy cast metal.

There are very few antique brass or copper pails or buckets, those pails that can be seen on the market are mostly of recent origin and probably imported from Turkey and the East.

Wine cisterns in copper or brass were used in many middle class homes in the eighteenth century for chilling the wine. Most of them were imported from Holland and are repoussé (i.e. raised in relief by hammering from behind or inside) decorated. There are many smaller round or oval containers in both brass and copper. These are jardinières or large vessels for flowers. Most of them are late nineteenth century or modern; the true wine cooler is large, over 24 inches wide, whilst the jardinières are only 12 to 18 inches wide. Period wine coolers had their decoration hammered into the sheet metal whilst the more recent jardinières are made of stamped out metal.

To open their wine bottles some brass corkscrews were made in the eighteenth century, but they are fairly rare.

Another small decorative piece of brass is the chestnut roaster. These are small shaped boxes on long handles and were used to roast the nuts in the fire. There are a few genuine nineteenth-century roasters about, but the bulk of those available were made for decoration not use, and date from the end of the nineteenth century or during the first quarter of the twentieth century when many reproductions were made.

Chapter 12

Lighting
and candlesticks

From the earliest times to the nineteenth century the only means of illumination was provided by the candle, oil lamp or rush light. We are accustomed to instant light at the touch of a switch, but there was no such luxury available to our fore-fathers.

Nor were any of the methods very effective and people had to make do with a limited smoky and short-lived light. Early to bed and early to rise was more than a prescription for good health, wisdom and riches. There was not much alternative unless you were rich enough to afford costly light into the night.

In our temperate climate, vegetables for oils did not grow so these had to be imported and were therefore expensive. Animal fats could be burnt in lamps, but they were very smoky and gave off little light. Lamps were thus a rather ineffective source of light and for many the alternative was to use rushes.

'Rushlight holders' are stands which hold the rush as it burns away. These rushes were cheap and plentiful. They were picked usually in mid-summer. The outer cover was then stripped off just leaving two thin bands to slow down the burning and to help keep the rush from bending. The peeled rushes were then diped in animal fat or tallow which was quickly absorbed into the porous structure. Such rushes would then burn well and gave a good clear light.

Great dexterity was achieved by people stripping rushes and even a blind woman could work at a great speed. Gilbert White calculated in 1789 that each rush burnt for about 30 minutes and that 1 lb of rushes, perhaps 600 or more, could be bought for 3/-; providing $5\frac{1}{2}$ hours of light for a farthing.

But even if they lasted this long it meant changing the rushes regularly and they were inclined to smoke heavily.

Candles were the best, but most costly, form of light. Provided they were regularly trimmed they gave off less smoke and they would each last several hours. For most people a single candle would have lit the parlour and would have guided them to bed. For the halls of the wealthy many dozens of candles gave a fine light.

Country folk used candles made from mutton fat or tallow and they made their own. The rich used beeswax and in the towns, candles would have been bought from the local chandler.

Candles could be made in several ways. They were cast in moulds, often of wood or tin, rolled from sheets of wax or hand dipped. This last method involved immersing the wick in the hot wax or fat, removing and allowing it to cool off a little, then repeating the process until a thick layer had been built up round the wick.

The candles were held in candlesticks and throughout the last two thousand years these have been made in most materials including brass and bronze.

Apart from their other advantages candles could be made more portable than rush lights. No one in his senses would carry a lighted lamp rush about the wooden house of the past whilst outside the first gust of wind would blow them out.

Lamps were used to protect the candle from the wind. Most lamps were made in iron or later, tin, but brass and copper examples are to be found. The light from the candle shone through a thin sheet of mica, horn, oiled paper or even glass.

Until the eighteenth century there were no real alternatives to lamps fuelled by animal or vegetable fats, rushes or candles ... Around 1780-1800 whale oil was imported and there were improvements in lamp design and in the 1840s slate oil was refined which with colza oil derived from rape seeds circa 1870, widened the choice of fuels for lamps. Then after the discovery of mineral oil in the USA, paraffin and other oils were increasingly used and soon drove out all other alternatives for fuelling lamps.

Although coal gas was first put to work in around 1805 it was neither safe nor serviceable until the 1860s as a form of domestic lighting. Electricity, first used in the 1840s was, after the invention of the filament bulb, an alternative in the 1870s, but its use in Britain was very limited until after the First World War.

After centuries of limited choice and poor light the use of mineral oils, gas and electricity revolutionised lighting and led to substantial changes in the way we live.

Apart from electricity all forms of lighting have to be lit by a flame. There were no lighters to respond to a flick of a finger! Setting aside the use of wood and bow, the only way of getting a light before the invention of matches was by flint, steel and tinder, a slow and cumbersome method.

Few lamps have survived other than those of the crusie form which hung on small backplates. Crusie lamps were particularly used in Scotland and the north of England. Care should, however, be taken as many have recently been imported from Spain. Most crusie lamps are in iron though a few may occur in bronze or even brass.

Rush light holders are also mostly in iron though a few have brass decoration. Rushlights now to be seen may date from the late seventeenth century into the early nineteenth. There may be some in brass, but I suspect these to be few and far between.

Candlesticks, however were made in great quantities over many hundreds of years and there are many forms still to be seen.

Prior to the establishment of the British brass industry, many brazen candlesticks were imported and as a consequence the early European and British styles have become inextricably mixed. The founders were casting bronze candlesticks from the Middle Ages, but it is not easy to tell these from their Continental brothers made at the same time.

Until the late Middle Ages the ruling class were French-speaking and owed much to French culture. As these were the people able to buy expensive bronze, most pieces were made to their Continental taste.

There were a few sixteenth century candlesticks either made in or used in this country, but all are rare and costly.

The first style of candlesticks to be made in this country independently of Europe are probably the trumpet-based candlesticks of the 1640s. These are so-called because of the obvious resemblance of the base to that musical instrument. Most trumpet-based candlesticks have a mid drip pan, called according to contemporary evidence, rather delightfully, the 'flower'. They have round bases and straight stems which are cast separately, turned and either riveted to the bases or fastened with a hand-cut screw thread. Trumpet-based candlesticks without the drip pan are also known.

All trumpet-based candlesticks are well made from good solid metal well-finished and are highly attractive.

In pewter, the dominant style of the late seventeenth century was the octagonal candlestick with a low drip pan and there is no equivalent in brass or bronze. But pewter, brass and bronze come together again with the knopped stems of the late seventeenth century.

Most brazen candlesticks of the period 1680-1710 have

100 A fine brass or latten trumpet-based candlestick with mid drip pan c. 1650. These candlesticks usually vary from 5 inches high to about 9 inches.

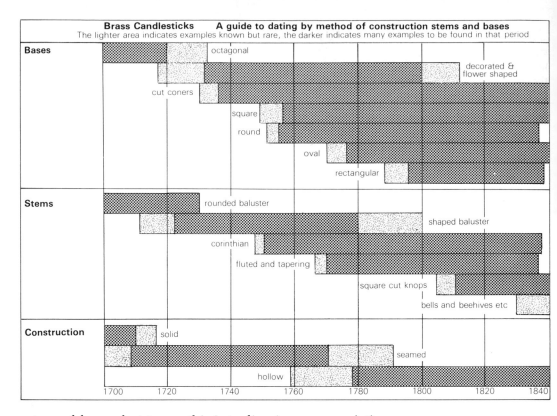

Brass Candlesticks   A guide to dating by method of construction stems and bases
The lighter area indicates examples known but rare, the darker indicates many examples to be found in that period

Bases
octagonal
decorated & flower shaped
cut coners
square
round
oval
rectangular

Stems
rounded baluster
shaped baluster
corinthian
fluted and tapering
square cut knops
bells and beehives etc

Construction
solid
seamed
hollow

| 1700 | 1720 | 1740 | 1760 | 1780 | 1800 | 1820 | 1840 |

octagonal bases, but to say this is to disguise many varieties, based on this general form. There are examples with more or fewer sides, bases made with prisms, fluted or with cut corners as well as other variations on the main theme.

The eighteenth century saw brass candlesticks drive out pewter and many hundreds of thousands of candlesticks were made in countless designs. Indeed the eighteenth century has been termed the 'age of candlelight'.

When we look at the products of the past it is natural that we should attempt to categorise them in order to understand better how they changed and developed. It is of course, we who make the categorisation and it is subjective. No craftsman at work in the early eighteenth century was bound by the rules that we try and establish.

Thus for every hypothesis that is advanced there is sure to be an exception, but if this is firmly borne in mind it is possible to divide the candlesticks of the eighteenth century into several distinct patterns and thus help to date many examples.

The criteria we shall examine are therefore:
1. Method of stem construction
2. Shape of the bases
3. Stem or column style

101 Three eighteenth-century brass candlesticks. Each is seamed. That on the left has an octagonal base, the other two have fluted or petal bases.

Each has its own contribution to make in dating candlesticks.

Before about 1700 all stems were cast solid and then turned off on a lathe. Although knops could be made, there was a technical difficulty in making them too elaborate. After 1700 the stems were cast in two separate parts and carefully seamed together. The stems could now be hollow or solid though solid stems are more frequently found. It was also easier to make more complex decorative knops in this fashion.

The final transition which occurred in the 1760-80 period was for hollow cast stems to be made in one piece. This speeded up production as the stems no longer had to be carefully seamed together. The change also made it possible to place a central rod up the inside of the stem so that the used candle could be pushed out. While the invention of the hollow cast stem is known to have been in use by 1760 most such candlesticks were probably made rather later in the century.

The shape of the bases which from 1700 to around 1730 were still basically octagonal underwent several subsequent changes all of which help us to date examples.

Gradually the octagonal base became more decorative and the straight lines are superseded with curves so that around 1730 the first of what we term the flower-based candlesticks appear. By 1750 these petal or flower bases are found with fluting or swirls rising to the stem and ape the very fine styles then being made in silver.

Square-based candlesticks make their appearance around 1760 but are probably uncommon for another twenty years and oval bases first appear about 1780.

Round-based candlesticks, though they appear very briefly *circa* 1700, do not reappear until the 1770s. Sometime in the early nineteenth century the octagonal base re-surfaces and

rectangular shaped bases are likewise from the first part of the nineteenth century onwards.

102 *Above:* A group of brass round-based candlesticks from the period 1760-1820.

Taking the last criteria next, the stems which were decorated with simple rounded knops in the period 1680-1710 are gradually made more decorative with shaped knops, smaller and larger balusters, knops with flutes and even 'wrythen' or twisted knops appear around 1750. In general the longer the eighteenth century lasted the more decorative the knops became until about 1760 when the first of the plain stem candlesticks re-appear. This was the Corinthian column candlestick and around 1780 stems with flutes, or which rise to a single knop—often an urn, appear. Square knops make their début around 1780, but those with cut corners or facets are after 1820. Knops in the form of a beehive or a bell are probably after 1850 whilst candlesticks with two twisted stems are from the late nineteenth century.

Within these general patterns there are naturally many dozens of variations and there are other features that change: the nature of the actual candle holder, the sconce or bobeche for example which was originally part of the stem and was then made separately for a period in the mid eighteenth century, only once more to be re-incorporated with the stem in the early nineteenth.

Using these 'watersheds' it is often possible to pinpoint the earliest date that a candlestick is likely to have been made.

To take an example. If you find a seamed Corinthian column candlestick, the method of manufacture suggests a date before 1780 and the column itself suggests a date after 1760. So the chances are that it is about 1760-80.

103 *Right:* Typical nineteenth-century brass candlesticks.

To take a further example; a petal-based candlestick with a hollow stem. The petal base suggests that it is likely to be mid-eighteenth century whereas the hollow stem proposes a date after 1760-80. It may therefore, be either a rather late example or perhaps made more recently and an examination for wear, turning etc. may well tell which it is.

There are of course, many other candlesticks whose form is not described within these hypothesis. There are for example in the early nineteenth century a group of candlesticks with telescopic stems, usually with round or square bases.

It is always possible that an item may have gone on being made in a particular style long after it has been assumed that this style went out of fashion. On the other hand it is not easy to sell yesterday's style in a market demanding the new fashions.

104 *Opposite bottom:* Late-eighteenth-century Corinthian column brass candlestick.

105 *Right:* Pair of early-nineteenth-century telescopic brass candlesticks. The example on the left has been extended to its maximum height.

106 *Far right:* Eighteenth-century brass candlestick with extractor operated from the side.

145

Such a fashion-conscious market existed in the eighteenth and nineteenth centuries so that some of the items in a style out of period may be genuine but many will be later copies.

As we have seen the hollow cast stem made possible the use of a centrally placed pusher to extract the used candle. In very early candlesticks this was done with the point of a knife using a hole filed away on the candle holder or later still drilled into it with a bit. Both methods did damage to knife and candleholder and were out of fashion in the seventeenth century.

With the arrival of seamed candlesticks that could be made hollow a pusher could be employed, but as the candlesticks were still riveted or threaded to their bases this had to be accomplished by cutting a rectangular hole in the side of the stem and fastening the pusher onto a small knop which could then be raised or lowered from outside. At the same time some straight-stemmed candlesticks with pushers were more simply made by bending a sheet of metal to form a circle and then seaming it together up one side.

In addition to the central pushers of the late eighteenth century onwards other more elaborate schemes were invented to get rid of the dead candle. Barlow was one of the many makers who obtained patents for extractors. His method was to have a small group of claws positioned within the candle holder turned by a knop outside. If the knops were turned in one way it gripped the candle more tightly, if turned in the opposite direction the grip was loosened and the candle pushed upwards. There are other variations on this theme.

The main styles of candlestick of the eighteenth century are illustrated on pp. 143-5.

A recent survey that I made of candlesticks on offer in the market place is given opposite. It shows that as you might expect, the vast majority of examples on sale are nineteenth

107 When candlesticks could be hollow cast it was more effective to put the pusher or extractor at the base of the candlestick.

108 Brass chamber candlestick, early nineteenth century.

146

century, but it also underlines just how rare early-eighteenth-century examples now are, so that when you come across them approach with caution. In undertaking this survey into candlesticks thought to be made after 1700 no attempt was made to date each example. The survey was into the method of construction, stem form and base shape. A sample of 400 candlesticks offered for sale in antique shops or sale rooms over a three-months period was examined.

Construction	%
Solid	1
Seamed	5
Hollow	89
Others	5
Stems	
Multi-knops	50
Round knops	15
Beehives	9
Fluted/tapering	8
Baluster	7
Straight/pushers	6
Corinthian	4
Spiral	1
Bases	
Square	42
Octagonal	30
Round	17
Oval rectangular	9
Petal/flower	2

As would be expected the method of construction, and the forms of knop, stem or bases most frequently found confirm that most candlesticks on the market are likely to have been made after 1760 and most will be nineteenth century.

Remember too that candlesticks in the Stuart and Georgian styles were being made in the twentieth century as reproductions. Whilst these may not fool an experienced collector the task of differentiating the good from the bad is complicated by the fact that recently some of the reproduction sticks have been returned to the workshop to have their rough cast bases neatly filed away and turned on a lathe so that they gain more of the appearance of old candlesticks. So look at the bases carefully. The turning of early sticks is very fine and now is usually worn smooth. Recent turning is usually wider apart and the ridges are plain to see.

Chamber-sticks, small round pans with a short stem and a

carrying ring handle were used when travelling from room to room. In eighteenth-century examples the stem is riveted to the base and later in the nineteenth century, screws are employed. Examples before the 1840s are made from heavy sheets of metal hammered into shape, those of more recent manufacture stamped out from sheets of thin brass or even soldered together.

Chamber-sticks with punched out fretted walls set at right angles to a flat base are also late Victorian or Edwardian. They are most attractive if well made.

In some cases the base incorporates a small box which was used to store the flint steel and tinder. Most of these candle-holders and flint boxes are eighteenth century.

Most people had to be content with the light from their rushes or a candle, but a few could afford to use several candles at once to light their drawing rooms. Chandeliers were in use from the medieval period onwards though few before the seventeenth century have endured.

Until the eighteenth century the bulk of chandeliers used in this country were imported from Flanders. Even when we did make them they were constructed in the Dutch 'taste'. Seventeenth-century chandeliers have wide-spread arms with the candle holders at the end, usually in two banks spread about a round central knop. In the next century the arms are made closer to the core and this is often oval or pear-shaped. Chandeliers with more than two banks of arms are also found more frequently in late rather than in earlier times.

The earliest wall fittings for candles were simple holders driven into the stone walls of the castle or the beams of the house. By the seventeenth century they are backed with a reflector. They are now called 'wall sconces' and they usually have rounded, fretted and engraved backplates with a polished central panel to reflect the light back into the room. The candles are held in two holders at the end of a pair of arms.

Brass wall sconces are rare, but many fine examples do exist. In the eighteenth century the candle holders are sometimes placed on a small tray at the base of the reflector and the backplate becomes rectangular, the top often tilted forwards to help reflect the light. Some examples were imported from Holland but others were made locally.

The large wall sconces with octagonal backplates, decorated with embossing, flowers and fruit with a second separate reflector added above, tilting down, are mostly from the Baltic area and were imported from the seventeenth to the nineteenth centuries.

109 Edwardian brass fretted chamber light with glass flue and snuffers. Brighton Museum.

110 An interesting brass wall sconce which has a scratch date of 1695.

148

111 A late Stuart pair of oak bellows with fine brass spout and applied brass decoration. Private collection.

112 *Left:* An Edwardian brass jardinière of typical wrythen form.

113 *Below:* A group of brass lighting implements. On the left a wall sconce and in the centre a tinder box with candle holder, both late seventeenth century. On the right a pair of early-eighteenth-century brass candlesticks.

114 *Opposite top:* A small collection of brass snuffers and doubters. Collection of the Curator of Horsham Museum.

115 *Opposite bottom:* Two mid-seventeenth-century candlesticks with trumpet bases. That on the left is in latten or brass. The example on the right, with a less pronounced base and heavier turning is in pewter.

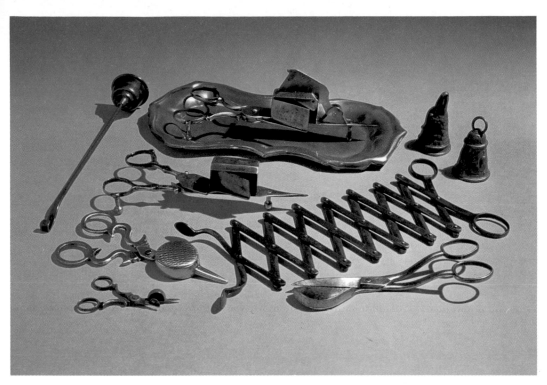

116 A student's lamp in brass,
the reflector helped to concentrate
the light of the single candle.
Nineteenth century.
Collection of the Curator
of Horsham Museum.

117 A mid nineteenth
century oil lamp of classical
form. The glass flue and
shade are missing.

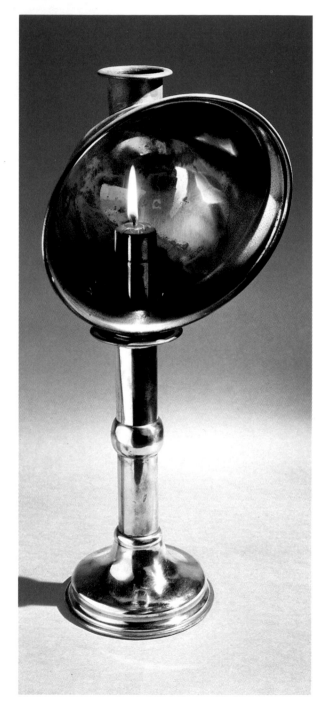

In the Victorian period large embossed wall sconces were made with tubular arms, often with embossed historic figures.

Collectors also ought to be warned that some fine early warming pan fronts, now separated from their pans have been married with arms to produce decorative wall sconces, but whilst they are often attractive they are marriages and their purpose has been altered and they have only a decorative not an antique value.

Lamps burning vegetable oil or animal fats gave a poor smokey light. The invention of Argand, a Swiss inventor of an improved lamp with a shade did much to improve the quality of the light and cut down on pollution. The Argand lamp was gradually adopted in this country and offered a twelve-fold improvement in brightness. The oils used were thick and did not flow from the reservoir easily, which was at first situated in the base. Other lamps were made with reservoirs just below the burner to reduce the distance the oil had to move and after Carcel had invented a clockwork powered pump, increasingly the oil was driven upwards rather than relying upon a gravity feed.

After 1800 whale oil was also available and from the 1840s slate oil was refined and gradually made available. After the discovery of mineral oil in the United States the next three decades saw the rapid expansion of oil lamps fuelled by kerosene or paraffin.

The speed of change is illustrated by the number of patents for new or improved lamps which were taken out and which averaged over eighty per year after the 1870s.

The next improvement was the use of the incandescent mantle for both gas and oil lamps.

There were many hundreds of lamps manufactured. A few mainly in brass, but many more combining pottery, glass or other materials with copper or brass. Many of the lamps and shades used in oil lamps were later to be matched on gas and electric fittings.

Oil lamps reached their peak in the 1880s though they continued in use for several decades, even after gas and electricity had reached most homes, as a stand-by system.

Although gas was first used for street lighting as early as 1805 it was not until after the incandescent mantle was available after 1884, that it became popular for lighting the home. The invention in 1838 of a process for making seamless brass tubes made possible the widespread use of gas and these tubes were also used for holding electric cables when electricity reached the home. Many wall or ceiling fittings are made with

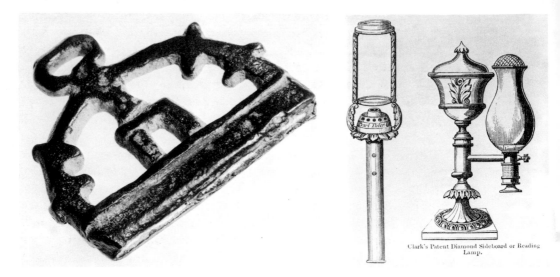

Clark's Patent Diamond Sideboard or Reading Lamp.

this brass tube often decorated at the time of manufacture.

So many different lamps were produced in such a short period that the task of codifying them is complex.

By 1900, in spite of gas and the appearance of electricity most homes would have been lit with oil lamps. But with another ten years the pattern was to change again.

A London store catalogue in the early years of this century devoted 6 pages to gas lamps, 10 to electricity, 19 to oil and $1\frac{1}{2}$ to candlesticks; giving an idea of the relative importance of the various forms of lighting on offer in Edwardian days. Twenty years before only oil lamps and candlesticks would have been significant.

For many household purposes the easy availability of a light was essential. Short of rubbing two sticks together most people had to make do with a flint, steel and tinder. By striking the steel against a flint sparks could be obtained and with skill and care a flame created by blowing on the smouldering cotton waste often used. It was common for 'strike, flint and floss' to be kept in a small box and some of these were made in copper or brass though tin and iron boxes were also popular. Few tinder boxes still contain their original equipment. Some of the tinder boxes were rounded and had a small candle on top and occasionally one finds quite large brass or copper candle holders with a box beneath, now usually empty.

A more efficient but costly mechanism was the mechanical pistol known as the 'Tinder pistol' or 'strike a light'. The mechanism used for this is the same as for a weapon, but instead of exploding the powder the spark is applied to the tinder. Many strikes have a small candleholder fixed to the end

118 *Left:* A bronze 'strike a light'; the flint was sandwiched between the two straight edges. Sixteenth century. Private collection.

119 *Above:* A brass lamp from the Great Exhibition of 1851. One of very many designs patented in the last half of the century.

154

so that when the flame has been coaxed it can be used to light a small candle. 'Strike a Lights' were at their most popular in the eighteenth century, and had wooden grips like the pistols of the period. In the late seventeenth century they mostly had metal ball and stem grips. Many 'pistol tinders' were made or decorated in brass and in fully working condition they are well worth seeking.

By the end of the eighteenth century there were experiments with matches; the earliest sulphur tipped and self-igniting were very dangerous. Later other types of inflammable material were employed but all were risky. The invention of the safety match was a great boon and by 1900 these provided the means of a light in most homes. Many different boxes and containers were in use during the nineteenth century for holding matches and many of these are in brass or decorated with copper or brass. By 1900 vesta stands were popular and these can be found in many forms.

When lit, candles needed trimming regularly if they were not to gutter, give off smoke and eventually die. Special instruments were used for this trimming called doubters or snuffers. Made in the form of a pair of scissors with a small box on one side for the trimmed wick and a sharp-edged blade to cut with on the other. Seventeenth-century brass examples are often beautifully engraved or embossed. Rather more eighteenth and nineteenth century examples will be seen, most in steel. Most snuffers after 1700 are plain.

120 Two early pistol strikes, both eighteenth century.

121 A group of late-nineteenth-century matchboxes or vesta boxes.

Early-eighteenth-century snuffers were also made with a small stand with a candlestick-like base and an aperture for fitting the snuffers where the candle would have been placed. Sets of candlesticks and snuffers were made, but most have long been parted.

Eighteenth-century snuffers with trays for them to stand upon were also popular. These trays had separate handles for carrying and rarely appear with their original snuffers. In the nineteenth century the trays no longer had a separate handle. Care must be taken with copper trays that they have not been plated at one time.

'Doubters' or 'extinguishers' were used for putting out the candle and thus avoiding the smoke that follows if the candle is blown out. Early doubters consisted of two small circular metal discs on a scissor-like device, similar in form to snuffers, but without a box to take the wick, or the blade. Later little conical devices were used to put over the top of lighted candles to extinguish them. These were often fitted to candlesticks, chamber sticks or supplied with snuffers and trays.

Copper and its alloys have played a significant role particularly in the centuries before the industrial revolution, in lighting our homes. They played their part too, in the constant struggle to help us keep warm as we will see in the next chapter.

122 Early-eighteenth-century snuffers and stand. These were often made ensuite with candlesticks of a similar design.

Chapter 13

Keeping warm

Cold was always an enemy. For centuries the harsh winters of Northern Europe were a constant challenge to survival.

Not only were there times when the winters were more severe than we face now, but the homes did little to keep out the pervasive cold. The wind drove in through the cracks and crannies of the lath and plaster houses or through the open windows, mostly only protected by wooden shutters. The damp rose up from the earthen floors or the chilly stone flags. Long woollen gowns or furs were some protection, but the key to survival was the open fire.

While the fire was centred in the middle of the room the family could all gather round, though the smoke, making its way slowly up to a hole in the roof, must have been a hazard. With the gradual adoption of the chimney the fire moved to the walls of the house and this discomfort must at least have been reduced.

Whilst wood was the principal fuel, the logs rested upon andirons, or fire dogs as they are usually known today. Later as the use of coal became more widespread, grates were used to hold the coals.

Iron was the material most used in the hearth though from the late seventeenth century onwards, brass and copper were used to brighten up the fireplace.

Even the provision of coal-burning grates in most eighteenth-century homes did not banish the cold. A Swedish observer in 1784 complained that rooms never rose above 50°F in winter and that during his visit he was always cold.

Whilst the fire was in the centre of the room the andirons were made to face in two directions, but with the adoption of the chimney the andirons faced outwards only. By the seventeenth century they started to be decorated with copper or brass, usually with cut and fretted sheet applied to the iron frame. As Fuller wrote in 1662 'brazen Andirons stand only for state'.

In the eighteenth century andirons were often made with

cast brass pillars. These are found in most styles with baluster knops, urn knops and columns being popular. Many andirons also had brass feet and the ball, ball and claw and the slipper shape are the most frequently found styles.

In the USA where the use of timber as a fuel continued right into the nineteenth century, andirons were still needed and many fine brass pairs were made up to the 1900s. In this country the use of coal drove out wood, already scarce by 1600 and the use of fire dogs went out of fashion during the eighteenth century, only to be revived this century with the reproduction of many fine pairs.

The fire backs, necessary to protect the back of the chimney and to reflect the heat of the fire into the room, were always made of iron.

The steady increase in the use of coal as a fuel led to the invention of the basket to hold the coals and provide sufficient draught to keep them burning brightly. At first the basket was probably suspended from the andirons, but later purpose built grates were made, combining andirons, firebacks and basket. The first grates gave the impression of being made up of several independent parts, but by the eighteenth century more harmonious grates were being constructed. Up to 1730 the grates had flat fronts, but later serpentine- and round-fronted grates became fashionable. Hardly any baskets or grates are wholly in copper or brass, but both materials are used to decorate the basically iron constructions.

By putting a plate of iron at the side of the grate or fire a hob was formed on which a kettle could be boiled or a stew cooked.

As with grates, the earliest stoves tend to look as if they are

123, 124 *Far left and centre:* A magnificent pair of seventeenth-century andirons with applied brass and enamel decoration. Victoria & Albert Museum, London.

125 *Above:* Pair of early-eighteenth-century brass andirons. A style much copied in the 1930s. Victoria & Albert Museum, London.

126 An interesting group of grates designed by Chippendale.

made up of several parts, but by the late eighteenth century designs begin to have a stylistic unity. Most stoves are in iron though again copper and brass were used as decoration.

Kitchen ranges were the next major development, incorporating ovens round the central fire with plates above for cooking on. These were popular in large kitchens by the 1850s though in the country cottage or industrial slum the grate and hob continued in use into this century.

Fenders were first used in the late seventeenth century, for preventing the logs from falling into the room, the earliest forms are large and straight, usually made of punch decorated or fretted sheet copper or brass applied to an iron frame. By the second quarter of the eighteenth century fenders with corners to hold them in place appear and the shapes become more fluid reflecting popular taste of the day. Many of the well-known furniture designers also worked designs for fenders. By the middle of the eighteenth century examples predominantly in copper or brass were made. Although a few early fenders have applied feet to give them greater stability it was not until the nineteenth century that this became common practice. Early fenders which were used with open fires or grates are usually large, often 4 or 5 feet long. Coal brought smaller grates and most nineteenth century fenders are small, by as much as one or two feet. Fenders range from 4 inches high to 10 inches or more and the taller examples are usually later.

127 Pierced eighteenth-century brass fender. Victoria & Albert Museum, London.

Large fire-guards with copper or brass wire mesh fronts, to prevent sparks flying into the room, appear around 1800 and were at the peak of popularity in the 1850-1900s.

The earliest fire tool was probably the two-pronged fork, needed as an alternative to singeing one's boots kicking the logs back into the fireplace! With coal grates other tools were needed; tongs or shovel for putting fuel onto the fire, a poker to stir and revitalise the fire and sometimes too, a brush was needed to sweep up the ash into the ember bucket to take away. The tongs and shovel were the earliest additions and later in the eighteenth century came the poker. Tongs usually had a disc terminal for gripping, those with claws are mostly Victorian or even later.

Most fire tools were basically of iron or steel, but there are a few fine brass pairs. Many examples have copper or brass handles. Eighteenth century tools are usually 24 to 28 inches long, made for the larger fireplaces of the day. The smaller Victorian fireplace brought shorter tools, but there were larger sets made even as late as the 1930s.

Early fire-irons had baluster or acorn knopped handles, but later perhaps reflecting the changing styles of candlesticks, more elaborate shaped knops became popular.

Sometimes you may find small pairs of brass tongs, 9 to 12 inches long. These were ember tongs, used for taking a small coal from the fire to light either a pipe or another fire. These were usually made with knopped handles. Beware of recent reproductions. Antique ember tongs should show considerable signs of wear and tear.

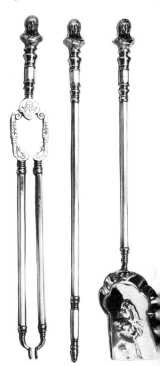

128 A fine set of brass fire tools with cast portraits of Queen Victoria *c.* 1870-90.

Bellows have been in use since medieval times; in the blacksmiths shops, in the brass workers forge and in the home. The increase in the supply of oxygen that a pair of bellows can provide makes a fire burn fiercely. Industrial bellows are often very large, but domestic bellows operated by hand mostly take the form that is still made today. Bellows are normally found in wood with leather used to make them air tight. Many have brass or copper nozzles, less frequently bellows are decorated with sheet copper or brass, fretted, engraved or embossed to add colour to the hearth. Early bellows have heavy large cast metal nozzles, but by the middle of the eighteenth century they become smaller and simpler. Another form of bellows which were used from 1750 onwards are mechanically operated by a wheel turned by hand which turns paddles to expel the air. These peat bellows, as they are now known, were popular in Ireland, but many were made in this country for use with coal fires. Like ordinary bellows these are mostly made of wood,

129 A late-seventeenth-century brass curfew.

130 Fine brass trivet dated 1668. Victoria & Albert Museum, London.

iron and leather with the brass or copper applied as decoration.

In the seventeenth century a device known to us today as a 'Curfew', a term derived from the French 'couvre feu' was used to place over the embers of a fire at night. There are fanciful stories of a curfew being applied to the fire at the curfew hour. This idea was the production of the nineteenth century romantic imagination. The curfew was one way of preventing sparks from flying into the room; remember how vulnerable the wooden homes of yesterday were to fire, or helping to keep the fire alive through the night. Most seventeenth or early-eighteenth-century curfews are Dutch in origin and are made in a rounded form embossed with patterns. They usually have a single handle made of the same metal. Later iron-handled curfews appear. They are also found with iron feet and with an iron grid across the back, presumably used in cooking. From this design came the better-known Dutch oven or Hastener with its sheet of metal reflecting back the heat of the fire to speed up the cooking of a joint or other food. Dutch ovens were imported into this country in the eighteenth century and many

161

of them were also made in this country. Mostly made of tin or iron, but some have copper or brass decoration.

Just as the Dutch oven was placed before the open fire to cook on so the footman or trivet was used as a stand on which a kettle or pan could be placed in front of the fire. Trivets were first used in the middle of the seventeenth century. There is a fine example in the Victoria and Albert Museum dated 1668. Most early trivets had three legs as on an uneven surface three legs are more stable than four. Their legs were normally made of iron to withstand the heat of the fire. The top is usually made of brass or copper or at least decorated with these metals. Trivets are decorated in a number of ways, fretted, with punch decoration or engraved. Most early trivets are small, only big enough to take a single pot or kettle. Later trivets tend to be larger.

The use of coal in the house meant that it had to be brought into the house and stored near the fire. At first, buckets were used and coal stored in baskets or copper vats. In the eighteenth century special coal buckets were designed and by the start of the nineteenth century these had evolved into the helmet style coal bucket we are all familiar with. Most of these were made in brass or copper.

131 Design for a coal bucket introduced in 1851.

From the 1850s gas was used increasingly in the home. The kitchens of the Reform Club in London had gas cookers as early as 1841 and water heating by gas appeared only a few years later, but was limited in use to the homes of the well-to-do until the twentieth century. The Great Exhibition of 1851 had several gas-fired stoves on view and in the 1870s their use increased. But even in 1900 it would still be true that most domestic heat was provided by a traditional fire burning a coal or wood fuel.

Electricity was not used for heating until this century.

Whereas much brass, copper and bronze is highly utilitarian, most used in the fireplace is decorative. It's not surprising that this is so for the gleam of the flames reflected on the brass or copper around the fire will cheer up even the bleakest winter evening.

Chapter 14

General household uses

Although they were especially important in the kitchen and dining room, things in brass, bronze and copper were to be found in profusion everywhere in the home.

We probably prize the warming pan above all other objects. For us they are highly decorative, but in the past they had a more serious purpose. No electric blanket, centrally heated room or rubber hot water bottle for our great-grandparents! They will not have found the task of defeating icy toes too easy, but the warming pan was reasonably effective. A round-lidded box on a long handle, it was filled with burning coals or charcoal and put into the bed to take off the chill. To our minds this sounds a lethal way of keeping warm, both dirty and risky, but until the stoneware bottle of the mid nineteenth century it was the only way of having a warm bed short of sending your spouse in first, to warm it up!

Sizes do vary, but as a rough guide most seventeenth century pans are above 12 inches in diameter and many up to 15 inches or so. Whereas pans from 1750 tend to be below 12 inches. The bowls on early pans are deeper than those used later.

Originally, the lid fitted close to the base, clipping neatly over it. In later examples, after about 1750, the lid rests on a step within the body of the pan. Where the lid is very much larger than the body, suspect a marriage.

A very few fine pans have turned and knopped brass handles and Dutch pans, imported in the eighteenth century in considerable numbers, often have steel handles. Most eighteenth century and later pans have turned wood handles.

Early warming pans have finely fretted fronts, often engraved with coats of arms or religious scenes. The frets were not just for decoration, but allowed the smoke to escape. During the eighteenth century fretting and engraving were replaced by punch decoration. By the nineteenth century pans are plainer, often with rows of punched holes on the lid. In Victorian times whilst warming pans were still in use in rural

132 Two fine brass warming pans. On the left a brass handled pan inscribed 'The Earle of Essex his arms'. On the right with a steel and brass handle a pan engraved and fretted with flowers and birds. Both seventeenth century. Victoria & Albert Museum, London.

133 An eighteenth-century copper pan, the lid fitting into the body.

areas they began to be made simply for decoration. A warming pan, frequently filled with hot coals, is going to show substantial signs of wear: the base holed, the lid cracked by heat and the hinge given way. Pristine pans are decorative and thus of more recent origin.

Bedrooms were not the only cold and draughty places in the house. As we have seen in the large rooms of the seventeenth and eighteenth century temperatures seldom rose to what we would now consider satisfactory levels and anyone working in a library, reading or doing embroidery in the living room was likely to get cold feet. Churches too, although heated were cold places in winter and sermons were longer than they are today. The gentleman would have to stamp his feet, but the lady could take advantage of a foot-warmer; a box filled with hot coals or charcoal, placed beneath her voluminous skirts. Most footwarmers were made in wood with a tin liner and perhaps not surprisingly few wooden footwarmers have survived undamaged. There are, however, some fine Dutch copper and brass ones, usually octagonal or square with fretted sides and decorated lid. Later examples are round with iron sides and plain copper or brass lids. Some of these may have been made in this country. The earliest ones that we can see date from around 1700 and by about 1820 they had gone out of fashion.

Before the nineteenth century metal beds were unknown, but by the 1850s servants were often provided with iron bedsteads and brass examples were becoming popular. A fine brass bed is very attractive and they command high prices today. Many of the Victorian patterns for brass bedsteads are being copied at the present time.

The night over, the task of preparing for the day also involved brass and copper utensils. Until this century most families would have had their morning wash in a hand basin of pottery, copper or brass and the hot water for washing and shaving came in a jug, often brass or copper.

Soap, an expensive commodity, was kept in small soap boxes frequently of copper or brass. Not until its cost dropped did we become more cavalier with it and let it melt away.

Bowls in bronze, copper and brass were in use from the earliest times, but few examples before the last decades of the seventeenth century will now be found. Bowls before 1700 or so have slightly rounded sides, rims parallel with the ground and pronounced central bosses similar to those seen on early pewter plates and dishes.

From about 1700 the sides become straighter and the rim tilts slightly upwards. The central boss remains till about 1730 when the base becomes flat.

Very similar styles of bowls were in use in Europe; indeed it is likely that most seventeenth century examples found in this country were made in Germany or Holland. Normandy bowls take a similar flat-bottomed form to our eighteenth century bowls but usually have decorated rims.

In recent years a number of Russian nineteenth-century bowls have been imported into this country; these have slightly concave sides and wide rims. Bowls are also to be

134 *Below:* Fine brass footwarmer. This is a Dutch piece but many similar footwarmers were made or used in this country, c. 1700-20.

135 *Right:* Domestic brass bowl with central boss. The boss which was out of fashion in pewter by 1660 continued in brass until about 1720, the date of this bowl. Used for most domestic purposes.

found which have been recently imported from the Middle East.

Nineteenth-century brass and copper bowls are less easily found than ones made in pottery. Pottery was cheaper. Bowls of this period are usually stamped out of sheet metal or shaped under pressure over a form, seldom cast.

Occasionally brass and copper bowls are found still with their nineteenth century jugs. There are a number of hot water jugs, some with lids, dating from 1870 onwards, still about. These take many forms, but are nearly all made of thin sheet metal with overlap or rolled seams. Few early soap boxes are English; most of the fine-fretted or plain-topped round boxes, with hinge and clip, are French. Later oval and round boxes, in thin sheet metal do still exist, some made for holding soap and the others for general domestic purposes.

Buckles were made in bronze from medieval times and from the mid eighteenth century buttons in brass, stamped out from sheets and decorated under the dies were made, in Birmingham particularly, in great quantities.

Drip-dry shirts are a blessing denied the housewife of the seventeenth century. For her smoothing she used a wooden board. By the 1700s irons were used. These had to be heated and therefore needed a small rest or stand to sit upon when not in use. Most early irons are of ferrous metal though occasionally you might find one decorated with brass. Many of the small stands, usually the shape of the iron, are made partly of brass. Another form of iron, the 'goffering' iron was used for shaping ruffles and flounces. The iron itself was ferrous, but the stand is usually made of brass. Goffering irons were in use from the eighteenth century but most that you will now see are nineteenth.

The next area to be examined is that of snuff-taking and tobacco smoking. Taking snuff, a mixture of tobacco and spices, inhaled up the nostril was a popular habit, especially amongst the more well-to-do. Cigarette smoking finally drove it out of fashion in the late nineteenth century. Gentlemen would carry their snuff in small decorated boxes and fine examples in silver, gold, agate and the like are much prized. There are also many brass and copper boxes, mostly nineteenth century. They come in all shapes, oval, round, square, rectangular, some plain, some decorated. Beware of boxes with early-eighteenth-century dates inscribed upon them for several factories were making such reproductions in the 1930s. The number of genuine eighteenth-century dated boxes is probably very small though fine examples are found in a

136 Sixteenth-century brass ring. Private collection.

number of collections.

The smoker used many different pieces of equipment; pipes for smoking, holders for storing the tobacco, cases for cigarettes, cutters for cigars, rests for pipes and pipe tampers.

Most pipes were made in clay up to the mid nineteenth century though a very few base metal pipes were around. Pipes made before the 1800s were all long-stemmed and are known as 'churchwarden's' pipes.

Most men had their own tobacco boxes. They are larger than we would now be likely to use; but were nevertheless easily fitted into the voluminous pockets of the eighteenth-century coat. Most of the boxes made before the 1750s are Dutch or German in origin. They are mostly rectangular in shape though there are a few oval boxes. Most are in brass, but you can also find them with copper sides and a brass lid, as well as all in copper. Many early boxes are decorated with embossed scenes. After about 1720 engraved boxes became popular. By the 1750s, boxes were being made in this country and the oval form became as popular as the older rectangular style. Boxes after 1750 tend to be plain, perhaps only inscribed with the owners name. In the 1800s personal tobacco boxes became smaller and much more common. They were still in use in the 1880s and plenty of genuine dated examples from the later Victorian period exist, some of the small personal boxes were also made in unusual shapes including the heart, some were fitted with combination locks to prevent the theft of the costly tobacco.

Table tobacco boxes were bulky objects. Found in most basic shapes they were made in a number of materials including lead, iron, pewter, copper and brass. Most of these boxes are nineteenth century. Many have finials representing human figures or animals on the lids and originally they all had lead or heavy metal pressers inside which rested on the tobacco to keep it moist and compact.

Some of the brass boxes of the 1850-1900 period are very elaborate, shaped in the form of medieval caskets, the sphinx or other unusual designs.

Pipe tampers were made in the nineteenth century, small objects, they were used to push the tobacco down into the bowl of the pipe. Many are in brass.

The cigarette was first smoked towards the end of the nineteenth century. The earliest cigarette boxes are thus late Victorian or Edwardian. Most are made in silver or plate, but a few brass or copper examples were made around the turn of the century. Cigar cutters are another piece of smoking equipment and some were made in or decorated with copper or brass.

Pipe rests, small sloping stands which were made to hold the pipe when lit but not being smoked, also occur from the late Victorian period and some of these were made in brass in the shape of boats or birds.

We are used to the fountain pen, the felt tip or the ball point; all with their own ink supply. Until the late nineteenth century the pen had to be dipped into the ink. Most people wrote with a quill until steel nibs came into fashion.

Ink stands, known as standishes were extensively used. They were basically small trays on which stood pots or containers. Most standishes have either square, rectangular, round or oval trays holding from three to five objects. One pot was for ink and another for sand used for drying the ink. This was called the 'paunce pot'. Additional containers, a bell, a stand for the quills and a holder for the taper might also be provided.

Some fine eighteenth-century standishes can be seen. Most from this period have three containers. The more elaborate sets with finely polished thinner containers and where screws have been used to fasten the pots to the stand are Victorian or later. The bulk of those seen today are less than 100 years old and with experience it will soon be possible to sort out those made by hand from the machine-made later examples.

For travelling scribes, pen cases holding a small pot for the ink, have been made from medieval times. Two very fine seventeenth-century dated examples made in Sheffield can be seen in the Victoria and Albert Museum. Later plainer examples were made but care should be taken with these as many pen cases were also made in the Middle East and these are very similar in style to those made in Europe.

Many other items for the house were made in brass and copper. Watch cases to fit the half-hunter watches, clock faces for the popular long case clocks, watch stands for placing the watch in at night, for example. The ladies used brass and copper thimbles, fed their birds in brass cages, kept their keys and scissors on brass chatelaines and rang brass bells for service. They kept their jewellery and face creams in brass and copper pots and boxes, put their plants and flowers in copper vases or pots, held back their curtains, which ran on brass poles, with brass curtain grips and kept the doors of the rooms open with brass 'porters'. The multiplicity of objects made in brass and copper is enormous. It is natural that most of these are nineteenth century and probably most from the last half of the century, for it was only when the demand for the essential equipment for the home had been filled by the brass and

137 Brass wax Jack. The thin wax wick was curled round the base on the narrow stem and fed up through the small candleholder which was opened and shut via the pincers on the right. This is from about 1830. Cambridge and County Folk Museum.

138 Hanging brass wall box. Larger examples were for candles or salt, smaller boxes for spices and various household objects. This is a nineteenth-century example.

139 Fifteenth century bronze personal seal. The engraving is especially interesting as it portrays two common metalworkers' tools; the hammer and pincers. Private collection.

copper smiths that the peripheral areas could be catered for.

In the eighteenth and nineteenth centuries there were several styles of hanging wall-boxes to be found about the home, most were in wood, but some were in copper and brass. Some were large enough to hold candles, others perhaps used for salt, spices, flour or other household materials.

In those rooms most frequently used, several candles will have been lit at any one time. After an hour or so these will have had to be replaced so there was a need for a ready supply of candles. Two principal forms of metal candle boxes were used. One basically rectangular with a hinged flat lid and a backplate for hanging on the wall, the other a round type also with a small backplate, but with a rounded hinged lid. Similar boxes were also used for other household purposes and it is not always easy to see at once the purpose of such a box. Very thin rolled sheet metal boxes with soldered or overlap seams are probably of recent origin for there were many reproductions being made in the 1920s.

Several pieces of brass would have been found in the study or library. For the sealing of letters and documents, and remember that envelopes are a recent invention, sealing wax was used. The flame needed to melt this wax was provided by a wax jack or taper candlestick. Most taper sticks are made like a very small candlestick and in the eighteenth century were made in all the popular styles. These are much rarer in the nineteenth century. Some of the Victorian small candlesticks are not taper sticks at all but made as toys for the nursery. Wax jacks are special devices which held not a small candle as with the taper stick, but a very much thinner and longer waxed thread. This was curled round the base of the stand and led up to the grip at the top, operated with finger and thumb. The heat of the flame would soften the waxed thread and allow it to be pulled through into position from time to time.

Jacks of a different form were in use in the 1700s, but most of those we now see from the late eighteenth or nineteenth century, take this form. Where the round bases are solid the jack is probably eighteenth century, where fretted from the nineteenth century.

Hand-cut seals in bronze have been made for ecclesiastical and personal use since the fourteenth century; occasionally these may be seen for sale. From the seventeenth century seals in wood, silver and brass were popular, but the majority of seals now available date from the nineteenth century. They carry crests from coats of arms or the owners initials and brass examples are not very common.

Appendix:
the level of survival

What are the chances that the candlestick on your mantlepiece is from the seventeenth century or that the warming pan on your great-aunt's wall is a genuine antique?

I have preached a certain scepticism throughout this book. Let me now try and show why this is necessary.

Anything made for use in the home will have a limited life. Some things will last for years, others will cease to be useful after a short period. We all know this only too well.

There is a natural life cycle for all things and domestic metalware is no exception. This will vary for individual objects within a class according to use and other factors.

Most brass and bronze objects will (probably) last a good many years before they break and have to be replaced. Pewter has a lower life expectancy.

Generally once the average life of an object has been reached there will be a steadily faster rate of depreciation until finally a plateau of what survives is achieved. Then it is kept apart, treated with a new respect as a survivor and its future more or less assured.

The speed of change can also be affected by dramatic changes in taste. A large proportion of gas and oil lamps will have been discarded in the 1920s with the widespread adoption of electricity. The two World Wars, with their calls for scrap for armaments must have speeded up the loss of many metal objects.

A series of theoretical life expectancy graphs are illustrated here. I think that you will accept that there is a natural life expectancy for most objects though it is not easy to quantify this.

For pewter we might expect a plate to last some twenty years on average, whereas brass and bronze cooking pots might survive for sixty or seventy years.

Now let us make an assumption. Let us assume that there is some domestic metal object which has been made over the last two hundred years at an even rate of production. That is each

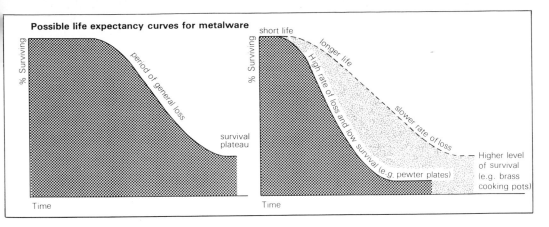

Possible life expectancy curves for metalware

% Surviving — period of general loss — survival plateau — Time

% Surviving — short life — longer life — High rate of loss and low survival (e.g. pewter plates) — slower rate of loss — Higher level of survival (e.g. brass cooking pots) — Time

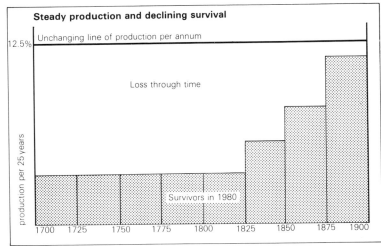

Steady production and declining survival

Unchanging line of production per annum

12.5%

Loss through time

production per 25 years

Survivors in 1980

1700 1725 1750 1775 1800 1825 1850 1875 1900

year the same number of items are made. Annually therefore, $\frac{1}{2}$ per cent of all those made will have been produced. So that for every 25-year period since 1700 to 1900 $12\frac{1}{2}$ per cent of all those items made will have been produced. But all will not have survived.

Let us next impose on this pattern of production a survival curve. Let us assume that the objects will all last 50 years and that thereafter they will be thrown away at a steady rate until a plateau of survival is reached which leaves us 20 per cent of the objects.

You will appreciate that this will change the proportion of the total we can expect to have lasted from each period. The chances of survival of those made in 1700-25 will be less than those made in 1875-1900.

The effect of this assumed rate of loss on the age of those that will have lasted is illustrated in a graph. Whereas $12\frac{1}{2}$ per cent were, we assumed, made between 1700-25 only one-fifth will

171

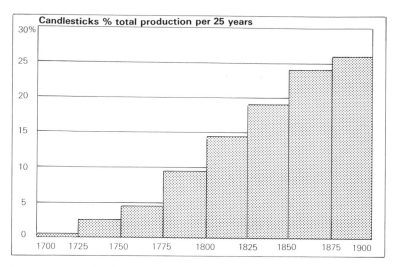

Candlesticks % total production per 25 years

have survived whereas of the similar amount made in the last quarter of the nineteenth century all will have lasted according to our theoretical analysis. This will considerably affect the age pattern of those that have endured. Only 7 per cent will now be over 175 years old; a very much smaller proportion than we started with.

Now let us turn nearer the real world; nothing has been made in equal proportions over 200 years. The population has risen eight-fold in this time. The amounts of copper used in industry rose ten times in the eighteenth century and at least eight times in the nineteenth. Not all of this will have been used in domestic metalware, but there will have been a very great increase in total production of brass objects for the house.

I have made an attempt to quantify the production of brass candlesticks in relative terms over the last 200 years. These theoretical production figures are illustrated.

You will see that I propose that less than $\frac{1}{2}$ per cent of all the candlesticks made will have been produced before 1725 whilst over half will come from after 1850.

These production figures do not yet take into account the natural losses that time brings. I assume here a life of some 75 years with a steady decline thereafter for another 85 years until a plateau of survival is reached at 15 per cent.

If these figures are applied to the production figures the picture will change considerably. The proportion of candlesticks made before 1725 will fall to around 0·14 per cent while candlesticks made after 1850 will now represent over 68 per cent of the total that survive.

It is possible to argue with the levels of production and the rate of decline and the final survival level, but the basic theory

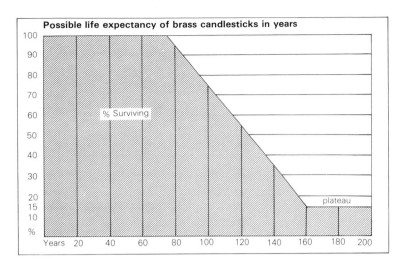

Possible life expectancy of brass candlesticks in years

% Surviving

plateau

Years 20 40 60 80 100 120 140 160 180 200

is I think clear.

If anything I think it is possible that I have underestimated the amount that is lost, leaving the plateau of survival still too high and again probably overestimated the levels of production in the eighteenth century.

Let us now take a single practical example. The exact figures must of course be taken with a degree of caution, as they are based on statistical assumptions as to the population, family size and ownership patterns of the population long before any reliable figures are available. We know from the study of inventories already mentioned in this book that where homes had pewter *circa* 1650-1700 there was on average $1\frac{1}{2}$ pewter candlesticks per house. Take the population at that date and eliminate half as being too poor to own such a possession, calculate the number of households and you will find that there were around 700,000 candlesticks in pewter in Britain, about 1700. Yet we know that less than 500 have survived; a level of survival of 0·07 per cent.

Brass and bronze will have had a longer active life and may endure in larger proportions than pewter.

The overall message is clear. Antiques more than 150 years old are uncommon and objects that have lasted from the 1700s are rare – the few who have managed to survive the tribulations of a long and active life.

Given this basic theoretical analysis it would be possible to count the numbers that have survived of certain objects and work backwards to the kind of levels that such a survival would imply. I suggest that in some fields, this might engender a certain anxiety! The numbers of 'seventeenth'-century coffers about imply a rather larger population than existed!

Glossary

Alloy A mixture of metals; an amalgam.

Andirons Fire dogs, bars of metal on feet used to rest logs on in the fireplace.

Antimony Bluish-white metallic element used in several alloys in small quantities.

Battery The term for copper and brass products that have been hammered by hand or under presses; 'battered' into sheet. Sometimes also used in the past as a general term for copper-alloy products.

Bismuth A reddish-white metallic element used in pewter and in other alloys.

Bobeché The loose fitting candleholder. In early candlesticks the holder or sconce was part of the candlestick, later it was made as a separate part and fitted loosely into the candlestick and was known as a bobeché (from the French).

Booge or Bouge The part of a plate or dish between the rim and the bottom or base; the side of the plate. The bouge traditionally had to be hammered in flatware manufacture in the pewter industry to give it additional strength.

Brass An alloy of copper and zinc; pure brass is mostly late eighteenth century or more modern. The earlier alloys of copper, sometimes called brass, usually contained other additional elements.

Brazen A description applied to copper alloys that have been cast; sometimes brass sometimes bronze or similar alloys.

Britannia metal A term used to describe the products of the last period of the pewter industry's eminence. Sometimes used to denote an alloy without lead (but with antimony) but as this was also strictly pewter, more exactly a method of manufacture of pewter using forms or patterns and shaping the material rather than by casting.

Bronze An alloy of copper and tin. Often also contained other materials.

Chock An item used to hold a piece of wood or metalware so that it can be turned on a lathe or formed round a pattern; the wedge or support used to prevent an object slipping off a machine.

Chopin A Scottish term (from the French) for a half Scottish pint or tappit hen (roughly 30 fl. ounces). Also used to describe the second size of tappit hen measure; of chopin capacity.

Copper The basic material used for making brass and bronze as well as an additional element in pewter.

Drip pan A rim or circle of metal sometimes placed half way up the candlestick (hence mid drip pan); sometimes nearer the base to catch the melted wax and prevent it from spreading onto the furniture.

Fine metal A term used in the pewter craft to denote the top quality tin alloy; usually a mixture of tin and copper with some other materials.

Flange The bent back edge of a plate or other item; a method of strengthening the construction of an item of pewter or copper alloy by turning the rim back on itself.

Gadrooned A form of decoration, usually cast, where the edges are shaped in scallops or fashioned into a series of convex curves.

Hollow ware A term used for items made in pewter and other materials which are not made in the flat; flagons, tankards etc.

Journeyman A fully qualified craftsman working as an employee for a master.

Latten A term used to describe copper alloys such as brass which have been hammered into sheet. Also loosely used to describe copper-alloy products that have been cast.

Lay Another pewterers' term denoting a lower quality material with lead as an addition to tin.

Mutchkin The quarter Scottish pint, similarly used as a name for the mutchkin, or half chopin (15 fl. ounces).

Ormolu A form of gilding; also an alloy for jewellery.

Pewter An alloy of tin with other elements such as lead, copper and later antimony.

Reeding A descriptive term used for the form of decoration mostly found on pewter plates and dishes. Sometimes incised into the rim, later cast with it. Brass and copper alloy items are also often reeded in this way.

Repoussé A form of decoration. The sheet metal is either cast or hammered so that the pattern is lifted on the front and hollow on the back of the object.

Sad ware A term for flat ware, or plates and dishes.

Sconce A reflecting back plate for a candleholder. Also a socket used to hold candles.

Trifle An expression identifying smaller less important items of pewter such as spoons and small boxes. Trifle metal was an alloy made of old pewter and tin suitable for such purposes. All three terms, *Fine metal*, *Lay metal* and *Trifle* had precise meanings, historically, in theory but in practice few alloys conform to any one description exactly.

Wrigglework The most famous form of decoration in British pewter, undertaken with a hammer and nail by a member of the work shop which made the object rather than by a professional.

Wrythen Another method of decoration where the shape of the body is formed, usually by casting, by twisting or distorting the line.

Index